Hores of Syringa

Brett Peterson

Acknowledgment

I want to thank my children and my whole family. Your love, patience, and support have helped me through my toughest times. Thank you for believing in me and for being by my side every step of the way.

CONTENTS

About the Author

Brett Peterson was born and raised in Idaho on a small farm with his family. He has owned several businesses in his life and taught school for over 20 years. He is retired and enjoying time with his family, and his dog and trying to give readers life events from the colorful events in his 70 years of life. His vivid views and stories hope to educate readers

Page Blank Intentionally

Chapter 1 – Mining Family

In the small town of McCall, families strive for the only thing they know: family strong. Old conservative towns in the Northwest mainly offer logging, mining, and agricultural opportunities, bringing traditions handed down from previous generations. There is little room or opportunity for large businesses or factories that provide steady local jobs, and people struggle when times are tough in traditional high-paying job areas. History has always proven that the West is a tough man's paradise or a weak man's hell. These traditions can be good, some not so good, but through it all, they imprint the heritage of the families.

The industries of mining and logging have one thing in common: they pay huge amounts of money when they're booming and then turn people into paupers as the boom crashes. As mining and logging booms start to subside, families slide into low-income status, not by their own fault but due to job insecurities and the inability to move elsewhere. With all low-income areas, healthcare—both physical and mental—starts to decline, leaving citizens to self-medicate with alcohol and drugs, which becomes drastically more common in these areas of poverty. This story shows the devastating loss of families because of these accepted forms of medication on generations of families.

Johnny is born into a mining family, and as much as he and his brothers try to escape the tough life of mining, it's all they know. Mining has always been a traveler's work: you go to where the boom is. Mines can dominate an area both physically and socially in the regions they consume. Most miners start employment at an early age, finding love along the way, more out of companionship and convenience than honest love.

Johnny, along with fellow miners in one copper mine, finds companionship among local Native American tribes in the area. The girls feel rescued, and the guys find a mate. It creates a lot of animosity among those involved, but at the end of the day, the miners offer what seems to be a better life for the Natives they are forming relationships. Most of the miners get married and move when mines close, causing a significant divide between the traditions of the two nationalities.

Johnny finds a young, beautiful Navajo girl, sweeps her off her feet, and makes her his wife. They start a family and continue traveling to different states and communities, never really feeling welcomed outside the mining camp. A lot of the mining families travel and stay together, as racism exists outside the mining camps. Mining camps don't offer luxuries like Marriott Hotels; average daily tasks are different for camp life: bathing, using the bathroom, and eating all involve every member of that mining society. Adults grow accustomed to this way of life, but children suffer from using community bathing houses, and restrooms, and facing the occasional comments from old, uncouth miners.

Like most kids who move from location to location, Johnny's children struggle to belong and make friends. They tend to put up walls in society and neglect self-care, becoming more likely to turn away from school, sports, and grades, and instead venture towards friendships in low places. They grow up learning how to take care of themselves — hunting, fishing, bathing in ponds or rivers, and cooking inside or outside the home.

One day, the children search for a way to protect their privacy and decide to bathe in the river by their house. Perhaps losing track of time, the girls — Melissa and Toto — get caught by the school bus, naked in the river, which causes embarrassment in school later that day

Johnny does his best to make his family function by working long, hard hours in the mine. He has little time or money for vacations, and at times doesn't see much of his family because of long day and night shifts. The only alone time he has is when he gets a few drinks with other mining buddies after work or on weekends, sometimes lasting all night. One can imagine this only complicates and widens the gap between the family and a sense of security — security from poverty, hatred, and vices.

As the children grow from young kids to teenagers, they find their own priorities that help them secure and support themselves. Some young boys just start working in the mines, accepting the ritual from boys to miners, good or bad, while young girls may find it harder to find decent employment at any age, so marrying into the crew is accepted as normal. With anything in life, norms don't always work for everyone's journey; resentment, freedom, and the desire to be one's own person often pull young people away from the community.

Chapter 2 – Leaving Camp

Johnny's family changes as time goes on, with two girls and two boys getting older and closer to leaving the nest. His smoking, drinking, and socializing only worsen with time. The family is tearing at the seams—Johnny's health is worsening, family time is even less than before, and his wife wants the love and romance she was promised years ago before she left the reservation.

The children do the only thing they know: having fun, partying, and drinking, with disregard for the glue that holds them together as a family. As this glue softens, emotions like hate, anger, loneliness, and jealousy rear their ugly heads. Johnny and his wife fight about his long nights at the bar, causing the kids to choose parental sides, isolate themselves, and distance themselves from the chaos.

Fights lead to affairs; affairs lead to community divides and animosity; and animosity leads to family separations. The mining community, along with ranchers, cowboys, and loggers, complicates the bar life for families and for people just moving through. Mines close, and miners find themselves moving like gypsies across the country. The typical families seem to move every 5 to 10 years, giving them a new start and, for a while, a sense of closeness again. Every move has its greatness; every move has its evils.

Johnny and his children witness a murder at the local bar when the kids are in elementary or junior high school. One of the local ranchers is killed in a fight. These Wild West activities shape young minds as to the norms of society, leading to poor choices in adulthood, and this upbringing is especially hard at the age of 12-16 years. It seems most mining towns are 100 years behind the norms of society; it's like watching an old Western gunfight series, with laws that sometimes seem medieval.

The oldest son goes to prison for repeated DWIs, the oldest daughter becomes pregnant, the younger brother joins the Air Force, and the youngest girl gets married and moves away.

This story is about the oldest daughter, Melissa—a smart, beautiful girl with baggage only Paris Hilton could imagine. Melissa falls into the reality of being a young, uneducated, lonely person, all while abusing drugs and alcohol. Her judgment is as poor as her financial status, and now, with a child coming into the world with no father, no insurance, no job, and no community support, things are about to get worse.

Melissa decides to venture out of her community and move into a world unknown to her upbringing. She must go to a place where employment will accept her and allow her to make enough to support not only herself but also a new mouth to feed. She moves to a resort town because they are less likely to judge people based on their nationality and financial status, and there is public transportation available, given the fact that she has no vehicle.

She finds employment cleaning condominiums and uses the bus to get to work. The pay isn't great, but it's work. She gets a room in a motel that has been converted into single-student housing. It's run-down and not compliant for hotel use, but it's a home for now. She survives for five months until she gives birth. Now, things really get challenging, as she has a new baby boy—she's alone and now has double the responsibility.

Chapter 3 – Young Life

Melissa names her son Kaden; he is healthy and eager to meet the world. Between daycare costs and added food, she struggles to make ends meet and decides to move back home. It gives her a chance to regroup, try to rekindle family ties, and apply for government assistance.

Her parents seem enlightened by the idea of being new grandparents and really try to be a family for the new grandson. After a few months, however, Melissa's parents fall back into their old groove of drinking, partying, and not providing good relations with the new baby.

One day, Melissa runs into a young miner who works with her father, and they strike up a conversation even though he is younger than her.

He tells her, "I saw you years ago and have always had a crush on you."

He's young but has a job mining and seems to be in love with her as they start this new relationship. Within a few months, he asks Melissa to marry him and take care of her and her new son.

She agrees, and Melissa and Bill marry quickly and decide to move to another town. Melissa's parents are furious.

"They will lose their pride and joy grandson," they say, "along with the government assistance."

Melissa tells them, "I will leave quietly and continue to stop by for visits, and you can keep receiving the food stamps."

This calms Johnny, who is having trouble working because of his health, and he agrees to help them move to their new home.

They move to a new town, where Bill gets a job mining in the hope of starting a new life with their family. As the months go on, Bill and Melissa fall into the pattern of drinking, drugs, and neglect accepted by their young age and community. Kaden gets left alone and neglected way too often because of this lifestyle.

Melissa meets a lot of new friends, friends that will consume her life for years to come. In just a few months, Bill's sister moves in with them, and Melissa will have her as a lifelong friend. However, at the time, this causes new problems— money being one of them, and a lack of alone time for the young couple being another. It's just a party house, and Melissa finds there's not much love, just people crashing for the night, sometimes for days and weeks.

To protect her son, Melissa decides to move out, leaving the one-year lease in her name, causing a large credit problem for her, one that she will discover years later. Melissa decides to leave the marriage despite the neglecting issues at hand and return to where she feels in control of her life—the ski town of McCall.

Melissa will deal with the current problems that could lead to lawsuits later, including expenses and damages. But as a young woman, her small family is more important to her than credit at the time.

Chapter 4 – Single Life

Melissa drives back to McCall in an old car she's purchased. Along with finding employment and an apartment, she also files for a divorce from Bill. She goes back to the cleaning company she had previously worked for and tries to start another chapter in her son's life. She works two jobs — cleaning houses and waitressing — to make ends meet, refusing to accept help.

Melissa has two things going for her. She is strong-willed and has learned at a young age to work like a miner. The other thing that God has gifted her is beauty; it helps her in everything she does and is a curse that is all wrapped up in one.

Once she gets settled, she talks to her younger sister, Toto, and asks her to move out to McCall. "Life is much better here," she says, "than in the small mining community you're currently living in."

After a bit of persuasion, Toto decides to move and finish her schooling in McCall to be close to her sister and young nephew. This makes it easier on Melissa — both for loneliness and having somebody to help with Kaden. It eases up her life to have self-time; just going out for the evening or going on a date keeps her mind from the depression of being a working mother.

The two sisters love each other and enjoy each other's company in times of need, but they also fight like cats and dogs when time allows — like a lot of families, I suppose. The biggest thorn in Melissa and Toto's relationship is beauty, something that haunts many families, male or female, and Johnny's daughters are no different.

Melissa is tall, skinny, and attractive, while Toto is short, pudgy, and not as beautiful. It is a combination that is a time bomb at any slight bump in the road. Melissa must dress down to keep focused on work, while Toto must dress up just to get a hello, and this, good or bad, affects both of their lives forever.

Toto's resentment towards life and Melissa's look pries daily at the way they function as sisters and as family. Since childhood, people have commented on Melissa's looks, and men have approached Melissa in the bar. Toto doesn't like the feeling of being the inferior sister. It drives Toto to acquire better jobs, drink less, and be less affected by the distraction of men's sexual attention—until depression sets in.

Toto blows up Melissa's mistakes in life while downplaying her own misdoings. Toto seems to take the family role of being better than the rest of the children, as one sibling is in jail, one has joined the Army to avoid jail time, and Melissa has an unwed child. Far from being a saint, Toto struts around like a 200-pound rooster, constantly demeaning Melissa for being a "drunken loser." It's Toto's way of feeling superior over her sister, but this never really beats the demons.

Melissa ignores most of the outside noise. She has heard it her whole life as a child, and she ignores Toto most of the time, living her own life. Besides, life seems to be going fine—Melissa works has enough money to survive and is giving her son a good living. Unfortunately, the past always seems to haunt us, and it's no different for Melissa. Years of domestic abuse, drugs, and alcohol are extremely hard to escape, especially when friends and family struggle with the same afflictions.

One night, Melissa receives a DWI on her way home from partying with friends, leaving Toto to take care of Kaden until she bails out a couple of days later. Toto is quite upset over Melissa's lack of parenting because of her alcohol consumption and refuses to babysit for her anymore for dating purposes.

This hits Melissa hard. She loses her driver's license for 30 days, must pay a large fine, and is in a position to lose her insurance. Once again, she is behind the eight ball, and this time the hole is harder to get out of. But perhaps her determination to survive will save Melissa and her son, Kaden.

She starts working nights as a waitress to make extra cash and to prevent herself from giving in to her desire for alcohol. Being Native American, she knows the struggle she will have to stay clean and away from alcohol, so she tries to fill her time with work and her son. Still, both alcohol and social interaction continue to haunt her; she is an introvert, and alcohol helps her warm up to meet people.

Most men are intimidated by her looks, don't want a "starter family," or are alcoholics themselves, giving Melissa a short list of options for love and happiness. Dating and finding love is a struggle for her, and loneliness always bites at her, feeding her desire to drink.

Because people talk and word gets around, the police begin to harass her because of her car's condition and her identity. It's a junker, and they find reasons to pull her over to check on her sobriety. It's a never-ending cycle—one she doesn't want but can't escape. It's only a matter of time before her insurance card runs out. When it does, hell will come to follow.

Chapter 5 – The Fix

One night, while working late, a man comes into the restaurant while Melissa is working as a cashier. It is late, only about 20 minutes before they close, so Melissa has to be both waitress and cashier. She takes his order and then, to help save time for cleanup, starts vacuuming the floor, as he is the only patron left in the building.

The man stops her and says, "It's rude to do that while I'm enjoying my dinner."

Upon leaving, the man pays for his dinner and holds the tip out in one hand, saying, "Next time you vacuum, this won't happen."

The man walks out, and Melissa thinks, *He is kind of an asshole for the comment*, but it's a ten-dollar tip.

The next night, the man comes back 20 minutes before closing, eats, leaves a tip, and departs. About a week later, Burt, the man from the restaurant, runs into Melissa at a convenience store. Burt barely recognizes her because she looks so different in uptown clothes compared to her restaurant uniform. It is a quick meeting, as Melissa is going out of town and in a hurry to meet up with friends. They exchange names, part, and go on with their evening.

A couple of days later, Burt comes back into the restaurant 20 minutes before closing, eats, and asks, "Would you like to go out sometime?"

Melissa gives him her sister's phone number and explains, "I don't have a home phone. Call my sister, and I'll check my work schedule."

Melissa usually spends time talking with Toto and uses the time to make phone calls, as she only has a pay phone in the lobby of her apartment.

A couple of days later, Burt calls to set up a date, and Melissa tells him, "Friday at 7:00 PM would be fine."

Things are getting worse for Melissa at this time with both vehicle maintenance and court proceedings. Her vehicle is very recognizable, and the police keep a watchful eye on her driving. She received a DWI ticket months earlier and has started to answer court proceedings. Her insurance card is good for six months, and that is just days from expiring. She knows she can't afford to acquire insurance with a state-enforced SR22.

While driving home on Friday, Melissa gets pulled over, as the police are sure she has no insurance. Without insurance, Idaho immediately suspends her driver's license. She is arrested and must bond out once again, although this time, she has a date in three hours.

The next day, fourteen hours after the proposed date, Melissa's boss bails her out, and she has promised to pay him back. In this period, cell phones have not been invented, and the U.S. mail won't make it for two weeks, so Burt won't be notified for days. Melissa now has a number of problems—no driver's license or insurance, no transportation, further debt, more court proceedings, and she's a date breaker.

Burt doesn't get too let down about getting ghosted; he's been stood up before—it's all in the world of dating—and he wonders why he received the sister's phone anyway. He's just gotten a divorce himself and is trying to start his life over, so dealing with any nonsense isn't in his cards. The other problem that Burt knows is that Melissa is ten years younger than him, so she probably just led him on to be nice. Burt can tell that Melissa is still young and still wants the occasional party life.

Melissa gets out of jail on Saturday morning and goes to work, as she knows she must pay her boss back. On her way home after her shift, the front ball joint fails, causing the car to fall onto the roadway without a tire. The car rides on the suspension, grinding both steel and asphalt as it moves along, which is a must-do, as she can't stop for anything, especially with the fear of the police. Melissa knows if she stops, the cops will come, and back to the cell, she goes — this time, it will get ugly. She drives the car three miles to her apartment, leaving a gouge in the asphalt highway all the way home. Like a bloodhound, anyone could track Melissa from Warm Springs to her front door.

Once home, she goes to the pay phone, calls her sister, and waits for Toto to bring Kaden home after he has spent all night with her. When Toto arrives, she informs Melissa that Burt had left a message, asking where she was for the date.

Melissa tells Toto, "I've been in jail and can no longer drive my car."

Toto scolds her, "Driving without insurance is illegal! I work for an attorney!"

The next day, Melissa calls Burt midmorning and apologizes, "I'm sorry for forgetting about the date. I had some things come up that consumed me."

She invites Burt over to swim that afternoon and to stay for dinner later in the evening.

Burt accepts the invite and asks, "Do you need anything from me?"

She jokes, "Swimsuit and car parts."

Burt shows up late in the afternoon and asks about her joke about car parts, and she shows him the car and the car issue. He laughs and says, "I can fix it in two seconds!"

They have a good time swimming in the condo pool, Burt meets Kaden, and they top the evening off with dinner.

The next day, Toto picks up Kaden and Melissa, takes Melissa to work, and takes Kaden for the day. Toto is living with a guy, and they have a car for transportation, but neither Toto nor her boyfriend wants to deal with Melissa's problems, including watching Kaden all the time. Their relationship is starting to deteriorate as sisters, as this is becoming more of a job than Toto wants to endure.

Without a car or driver's license, Melissa's life is going to go bad quickly; everyone knows the chain reaction that follows with transportation issues in America. Melissa can use the public bus to run around town but not to go out of town for work or pick up her son.

Burt goes by the auto parts store and purchases a ball joint for Melissa's car. He grabs his tools and proceeds to her apartment to repair it. Burt laughs as he sees how far she drove with a broken ball joint and admires the skill needed to drive a car that far on three wheels.

"It's an easy fix for any mechanic, in the shop or on the street," Burt says, and in less than an hour, Melissa's car is fixed and ready.

Burt goes to dinner on his normal routine, twenty minutes before the restaurant closes, and informs Melissa, "Your car has been repaired."

She is very appreciative and thanks him for his good deed, saying, "Dinner is on me."

Melissa doesn't say anything about her problems with the law and the fact that she can't drive. Luckily, Burt offers her a ride home if needed.

She accepts, adding, "If we can swing by to pick up Kaden at my sister's house."

Burt agrees and ends up meeting Melissa's sister and boyfriend before dropping her and her son off at the apartment. Burt doesn't know any of her problems, thinking that the ball joint and old vehicle are her biggest hurdles. That's not the case by a long way, but Melissa is great with secrets — something she has been good at her whole life. When drinking, cheating, poaching, and lying are daily occurrences as a child, you learn secrets.

That week, Melissa invites Burt over to go swimming, as she is at home with Kaden in the housing complex. Melissa is staying close to home and has a driver's license problem. She's normally an out-and-about girl, but now that will have to wait. Burt goes over to swim, throws Kaden around the swimming pool, and sits in the hot tub for a while with Melissa. After an afternoon in the water, they go out to dinner in town, return, and Burt heads out for home.

They have a good time swimming and dining, and Kaden really likes the attention and having somebody to play with. Burt can tell he's been neglected for attention.

Later the next week, Burt is driving down the highway when he notices a woman standing on a car hood parked on the side of the road, in a dress, jumping up and down. It's Melissa, and her hood came open while driving because she added oil and forgot to latch it correctly. Burt is towing a trailer and cannot pull over on this highway, so he hopes she has it handled.

Later that evening, when Burt comes to the restaurant to eat, Melissa tells him what had happened that day and that she had to go to court earlier in the day because of a lack of insurance. They both laugh.

"It's not every day you see a woman in a skirt and heels jumping on a hood to make it latch," Burt says.

He then asks, "Would you like to try another day for a date later in the week?"

She accepts and tells Burt, "Pick me up at 7 PM."

They go out to dinner, pick up Kaden at the babysitter's, and escort them home to Melissa's apartment complex.

Burt asks, "Why did you get a babysitter?"

Melissa explains, "My sister is pregnant and wasn't feeling like watching Kaden much."

Burt says, "I have my son most weekends, and Kaden could play with him, saving you money on daycare."

She agrees and finds it kind of different that a guy would accept her and her child, as most men her age would treat them differently.

As luck would have it, Melissa gets pulled over again. This time, the police impound her car, but because her son is in the car, they don't arrest her. Now she is down on luck, down a car, and has no way to get to work. She calls her sister Toto, and although her sister isn't happy, Toto gives her a ride home and asks, "What are your plans now that you have no car?"

Melissa calls Burt and tells him about the day she did not have insurance and how lucky she feels not to be arrested. Burt agrees. Burt is on his way to pick up his son and asks, "Do you and Kaden want to ride along?"

It is a two-hour trip, but he promises, "I'll buy dinner."

They agree. After they get back from picking up William, Burt suggests, "Why don't you borrow my extra car for a couple of weeks to give you a chance to regroup? Perhaps the cops won't know you're driving my car."

Melissa starts driving a sports car with tinted windows, and it works out great. She saves money and is less worried about getting pulled over.

Chapter 6 – Bait and Switch

A couple of weeks later, Toto is getting married, and Melissa invites Burt to attend the wedding with her. Over the next few months, Melissa and Burt start seeing each other often, sometimes every day, as Burt spends a lot of time babysitting Kaden, even while he is working. They enjoy the outdoors together, doing activities that remind Melissa of the good moments of her youth, and most importantly, her son Kaden loves the attention. Kaden has someone to teach him about camping, hunting, jet skiing, and growing up in general. He enjoys spending time with Burt's son, William; they are just one year apart in age, so everything they do feels like they are brothers.

Melissa enjoys the time spent together, but due to her past, she struggles with trust, love, and relationships with men, which keeps her at a distance. As summer ends and hunting season approaches in Idaho, Burt plans a two-week hunting trip with his friends. Before leaving, he tells Kaden, "If your mom brings you to camp in a week, you can hang out for the weekend until we get back."

The week goes by, and at one point, Burt runs into Melissa's father, Johnny, at a gas station. They had only met each other at Toto's wedding two months earlier. Johnny introduces himself to Burt's hunting buddies and says, "I can only drive the roads to hunt because of my health, so if you run into elk, kill one for me."

They all laugh, but Johnny insists, "I'm serious," and hands over his elk tag. "I need the meat to feed my family."

By the time the weekend comes, Burt has been at the hunting camp for over eight days. Kaden is elated to attend the hunt, but Melissa feels differently; she is upset that Burt hasn't spoken to her all week. Since her father knows the area well, he leads her and Kaden to the hunting camp on Saturday. Elk are hanging at camp from the week's hunt, including one for Johnny.

Kaden is excited to be at the camp and overjoyed with all the animals Burt and his friends have hunted. After the initial chaos settles down, Melissa expresses her frustration to Burt.

"I'm upset that you've been hunting all week with no regard for my well-being," she says. "I had no idea if you were alive or if you had been at the bars all week."

She continues, "I don't want to see you anymore because of this. I can't be with someone I don't trust. Just drop Kaden off when the weekend is over."

Johnny, who is intoxicated, intervenes and says, "You're an idiot, Melissa. Why can't you just admit you like him and quit being a dumb bitch? Burt has done nothing to be untrustworthy."

Melissa, irritated by her father, helps load the elk into his trunk and prepares to leave for home. Burt tells her, "I'll be back late Sunday afternoon after we finish preparing the game for the meat locker and allow Kaden to spend the night in camp."

Once Burt and his hunting friends return home with Kaden, they find that Melissa has cooked dinner for them, acting as though nothing has happened. This is her way of coping with the scene at camp. Her childhood has built walls that make it difficult for her to reason, mostly due to alcohol use from a young age and growing up around others who were the same. Melissa is smart and wants the best in life, yet addiction is always there, knocking at the door, despite her efforts to rid herself of the "monkey."

Burt questions the scene in his mind but writes it off as a one-time event that will heal with his continued support. In the next few months, things go well, both personally and with friends and family. However, living a straight and narrow path causes boredom for Melissa, who struggles with her addictive tendencies. Going out, partying, and hanging with girlfriends all have their vices, and breaking those habits is hard, even under the best of circumstances.

As the months roll by, winter weather limits outdoor activities like camping, hunting, and swimming. For Thanksgiving, Burt decides to visit his sister in Arizona, where the weather is nicer, and he hasn't seen her in a couple of years. He invites Melissa and Kaden to come along, and they are excited to join him. They pick up Burt's son, William, and start their journey to Arizona for a week-long vacation.

On the first day, they stay in Winnemucca, Nevada, spending the next day in Humboldt National Park, and end up in Las Vegas by the evening. The boys are mesmerized by the lights and casinos, especially the Excalibur, where they get a room for the night. The next day, they head for the Grand Canyon and tour Hoover Dam in the afternoon, hoping to reach Phoenix by nightfall, which they do.

They meet Burt's sister, Hide, along with her cats, which both boys love playing with since they both adore animals. The following day, Hide joins them at the Phoenix Zoo for a long day filled with exploring and seeing a variety of animals. The next day, they spend time at Hide's ranch, fixing things and relaxing with her horses, preparing for their journey back home. On the final day, they leave for home after having a great vacation—one that the boys will remember for a lifetime. Melissa and Burt get along better than ever, and Melissa has not had a single drink the entire trip. It almost seems like they are two parents for the two boys.

Back home, things are going well except for the looming court cases that Melissa faces, which are something she wants to avoid. Drinking doesn't help matters, but Melissa needs $1,500 to stay out of jail, and waiting will only make things worse. She borrows the money from Burt by giving him a check to hold for ten days, hoping she can make enough in that time to pay him back. Melissa knows it will take a miracle to come up with that kind of money, but her life experiences haven't prepared her for the consequences of breaking the law in America—something she should have learned from her brother, who went to jail for his abuse of alcohol and driving.

Burt can tell she is stressed and suggests, "Why don't you take the weekend off and come with me to my sister's wedding in Salem, Oregon?"

Melissa thinks that by going, her troubles will somehow magically disappear, so she agrees, but with a condition.

"No kids," she insists.

Perhaps by acting like a couple, just the two of them, they can kindle a love strong enough to overcome her problems.

They have a wonderful time all weekend long, except for the overindulgent drinking with Burt's future brother-in-law. He is a large man with a liver like a tank, and Melissa tries to keep up with him drink for drink, only to find herself unable to handle it. At the wedding party dinner, Melissa becomes extremely intoxicated and passes out face-first in her food, forcing Burt to carry her to their motel room. It is embarrassing for Burt, but his brother laughs it off, saying, "I've done that before, and even drove home afterward!"

For the first time, Burt realizes that Melissa struggles to understand her own limits with alcohol and that she can easily put herself in unsafe situations.

Chapter 7 – Commitment

To make things worse, Burt receives a notice that the check Melissa gave him is no good. He decides to wait until Melissa brings it up, as a sort of test of trust. Weeks go by, and Melissa doesn't mention it. Around the same time, she discovers she is pregnant. She isn't particularly happy, but Kaden and her family are excited about the prospect of another child.

Burt and Melissa discuss the matter and decide to get married. They agree to do it quickly, in Nevada. Burt informs her, "No cigarettes or alcohol during this pregnancy."

Over the weekend, the two of them go to Winnemucca and tie the knot. Melissa feels torn between the life of motherhood — full of responsibilities like caring for her child, working, and all the "boring" aspects — and the single life she used to lead, filled with alcohol and freedom. One big problem is that partying costs money, but so does staying out of jail. The answer seems obvious, but she isn't ready to admit it to herself.

She puts her best foot forward, stops smoking, tells her friends she is expecting, and decides to give up drinking. She works evenings, comes home, and prepares for the baby, which keeps her mind off the bar scene — something she hadn't stepped into since she was young and after having her first child.

Burt doesn't know the family history very well. It has been a short time to learn all the ins and outs of any family, let alone this one. Melissa's mother, Betsy, is Navajo and lived her early life in Arizona, where a lot of government testing had been conducted; she developed cancer. Betsy has experienced ups and downs, but now she is in the final stages and is going to die.

After staying with Toto for just a week, Betsy passes away. It is devastating for the kids, but Johnny is at a complete loss without her. Melissa focuses on her pregnancy; she works, cooks for her family, and even includes her father at times. She is a good cook, as she has been raised that way, probably doing a lot of the caretaking for her family at a young age.

Even her brother comes for their mother's funeral and stays for a few weeks to visit and party with friends and family. During his visit, he receives a DWI after leaving the bar. Melissa begs Burt, "Please, bail him out so he can make it back to work in Nevada."

Reluctantly, Burt complies.

At seven months into the pregnancy, Melissa and Burt go to the doctor for a routine checkup. They do some tests and discuss the rising costs of healthcare. Burt has a few words with the doctor, saying, "The cost of having a baby in this resort town has tripled since my son was born just three or four years ago."

The doctor suggests, "It might be better to find a doctor you feel more comfortable with."

After considering the suggestion, they decide to find another doctor in Boise. They schedule an appointment for the next week, but before they can attend it, a nurse calls with grim news.

"The baby is going to be stillborn," she says.

This changes everything. Melissa spirals into depression, which lasts a month. The only way out for her is alcohol. It doesn't solve her problems, but it lets her forget them for a while. She doesn't leave the house for weeks and just stays in bed. Burt doesn't know how to help her. He has never dealt with anything like this before, and for Melissa, the answer to dealing with pain has always been to get drunk and forget. Her sister, Toto, starts coming over and taking her out to visit girlfriends for a few drinks.

It isn't the remedy Burt had hoped for, but at least it gets her out of the house and might help lift her from her depression. Burt doesn't like the new situation but understands how devastating recent events have been. This approach seems to be helping, even if it isn't ideal. Burt also asks one of his friends if he could hire Melissa to answer phones at his title business since she lost her jobs due to absenteeism.

His friend agrees, saying, "I could use a secretary. Maybe it could work out to be something more in a few years."

When Burt suggests the job to Melissa, she is a little nervous about it but agrees to go in for an interview. She goes in and is excited when she gets the job. She is thrilled because she has never imagined this type of career opportunity for herself.

Thanks to Burt's great relationship with her new boss, Dave doesn't even ask about Melissa's past, work experience, or education. In Dave's mind, being married to Burt is enough. Melissa's attractiveness and bubbly personality are both gifts and curses. Those close to her understand how introverted and shy she is, but she is also a good worker—something her parents taught her: to work hard.

Melissa isn't just a drinker; she is an alcoholic. She functions better than most employees during the day, but the call of the evening is her demon. Burt observes the problem; he sees the "pink elephant in the room," but it somehow seems to fit the décor of their lives.

Burt is happy with her new employment. She is out of her depression and seems committed to making it work. She comes home at 5:30 each day, and with her father staying in the house, she seems to take on the role of being a mother again. Her new job is going well. Everyone loves her, and the manager keeps adding more responsibilities beyond just answering the phone. She even takes the company car to retrieve documents from the courthouse.

One day, her boss asks, "Can I get a copy of your driver's license for the insurance company? It's required to drive the company vehicles."

Melissa hands it over, but fear grips her. She knows that in a day or two, bad news will follow. Just as she expects, the next day her boss asks, "Did you know your driver's license is void?"

She answers, "Yes."

Her day crumbles after that. She goes home and cries, but the crying soon turns to alcohol, and she gets drunk with her father, passing out by the time Burt gets home. A reckoning is about to come.

Chapter 8 – The Reckoning

Burt gets home to find Melissa passed out, while Johnny is still drinking. Johnny suggests, "Melissa had a rough day, losing her job."

Johnny continues, "I've enjoyed your hospitality, Burt, and I know you're right about the drinking. Thank you for everything you've done for both Melissa and Kaden." He adds, "I'll head home in a couple of weeks to try and help minimize the problems here."

Johnny admits, "I know alcohol has been a problem for me and my family, but at this point in life, I can't quit after 60 years of abuse."

Burt responds, "I just can't have alcohol around the boys, Johnny. They're only five years old, and they don't deserve this kind of upbringing."

Johnny agrees, "I promise not to drink or smoke in the house, and I'll head home next weekend." He then leaves for the saloon, saying, "I'll be home later tonight."

A few hours later, Melissa wakes up and asks, "Where's my father?"

For some reason, she is irritated with Burt, even though he has nothing to do with the problems of the day.

Burt suggests, "Why don't you call a couple of the local bars to try and locate him?"

Melissa does and then tells Burt, "I'm going to pick him up."

Burt recommends, "Why don't you just call him a cab at this late hour?"

But Melissa refuses. About an hour later, she returns home with her father. Burt has started doing billing and paperwork for the business since it is quiet and the boys are asleep.

Melissa has had a few drinks at the bar before leaving and starts badgering Burt in the office. "Finish the billing tomorrow," she insists.

Burt replies, "I'll be done in just a few minutes."

Annoyed, Melissa goes to the kitchen, fills a cup with water, and throws it at Burt and the keyboard, irritating him. Burt tries to stay calm and says, "The boys are asleep, Melissa. I don't want to wake them, so you need to settle down and go to bed."

This infuriates Melissa. She grabs the coffee cup and smashes it against his head. Burt has had enough—he goes for the phone and calls the police.

"You're such an asshole for calling the police!" Melissa screams. The situation brings back memories from her childhood that haunt her, and she retreats to the bedroom.

A few minutes later, the police arrive, waking up the entire house. The male officers take Melissa outside, while a female officer stays inside with Burt and Johnny to hear their side of the story. Melissa reacts the only way she knows—retaliating. She strikes one of the officers and runs down the highway, leaving the rest of the family in the house.

Kaden watches from the living room window, giving a play-by-play of what he sees as Melissa is arrested for assaulting an officer right in front of the boys. Johnny tries to explain, "Your mom was wrong for drinking too much, getting stupid, and hitting a cop." Burt knows it will just end up costing him more money.

The next day, Burt goes to bail her out. "I want the full story, top to bottom, or you can sit in jail," he tells her. "I deserve that from you."

Melissa agrees and pleads, "Please, just get me out. Without your help, I fear I may end up in prison."

Burt bails her out and tells her, "You need to think of others besides yourself." It is a lecture she doesn't want to hear.

Melissa doesn't like being in the spotlight, nor does she want to take responsibility for her wrongdoings. She isn't comfortable with it; her usual approach is to run away and hide from her problems. Under all the pressure, Melissa promises to find out who Kaden's father is, knowing it troubles both Burt and Kaden. She explains about receiving the DWI, losing her license, and driving without insurance—all of it connected to alcohol. Talking about it brings out the truth, but that doesn't mean it is the end of her problems. She will have to work on each issue to resolve it.

They talk about the future, what each of them wants, and most of it revolves around the boys. "I loved my job," Melissa says, "but now, without a license, I'll have to go back to waitressing—a job I really don't like."

Burt assures her, "I'll see what I can do. Just stay positive for now, and let's focus on each other and the boys."

They go to lunch and then return home. When they arrive, Toto is waiting to see what is going on, as she has spoken to their father, Johnny. Toto is irritated with Burt for having Melissa arrested and thrown in jail.

"Burt, I can't believe you did this to her!" Toto exclaims angrily.

Burt realizes, *Blood is thicker than fact.* Melissa and Toto then load up in the car to find their father. They find Johnny at a local bar, and they both go in to talk about how "awful" Burt is.

Johnny buys them a beer and begins to talk. "Look, last night was not Burt's fault at all," he says. "I witnessed the whole thing."

Johnny tries to explain, "Melissa, you were drunk and took it out on Burt."

While driving around town looking for their father, Melissa had suggested, "Maybe Burt just beat me up, and when the cops showed up, they arrested me for being drunk because they're his friends."

After Johnny defends Burt, Melissa and Toto boycott their father, feeling betrayed. "You've teamed up with the devil, Dad. You've chosen Burt over us," Melissa shouts as they leave.

Burt, who has gone looking for the family, walks into the bar to find Johnny sitting alone, looking sad that his daughters have disowned him for speaking the truth. Burt sits beside him, and Johnny offers, "Want a drink?"

Burt accepts, knowing Johnny is upset. They finish their drink and head home, only to find out that Johnny is too drunk to drive. He runs into the garage as he pulls into the driveway. Meanwhile, Melissa and Toto go to other bars and return home a few hours later. Melissa completely loses it when she finds out Burt has shared a drink with her father, who had been sober for 12 years.

"You didn't even have a drink at our wedding!" she screams.

Burt responds, "I only drink on special occasions." The boys, being funny and observant, chime in, "And that's how the fight got started!"

The next day, Johnny decides he has overstayed his welcome. He says goodbye to the boys and Melissa, packs up his Buick, and leaves town.

The following weekend, Melissa wants to see her father to apologize and make things right. Burt decides to take the camper so they can camp along the way, as it is quite a drive and would give them a place to sleep. Burt, Melissa, and the boys leave late on Friday, so they stay along the river at a small pull-off to avoid falling asleep at the wheel, about 100 miles from Johnny's place.

Around 6 AM, a police officer knocks on their camper door. The officer explains, "Johnny passed away from a heart attack during the night, about four hours ago."

Melissa breaks down. The weight of her last words and unresolved feelings toward her father makes this especially difficult. Burt tries to console her, saying, "Your father liked who he liked, Melissa. Daily quarrels had nothing to do with it."

Growing up, Melissa had almost always stuck by her mother's side, but Burt can tell the loss of her father affects her much more deeply. Johnny had been the rock of the family, even though most people saw him as a drunk, an abuser, and the bad guy. Over the next few months, Burt learns that it was really the opposite with his in-laws' marriage—judging a book by its cover was misleading in this case.

Burt and Johnny had shared a great relationship in the time they had known each other, and Burt never really knows why Johnny respected him so much, other than for taking care of his grandson, Kaden. Melissa probably appreciates her father standing up for Burt, feeling like she had made the right choice in love for once. It is the opposite for Toto—she hates Burt and the relationship her father had with him. She feels that Burt is sabotaging the family, making it seem as though alcohol affects them all.

It is strange thinking for Burt, but he always says he has enough friends when anyone calls him an "asshole." Johnny's death is the loss of a friend and the bridge for Melissa's relationship with Burt. Burt knows he has to help her through this next challenge, so he does what he can for her in the coming weeks. Johnny has left his house and property to Kaden after his death, which is something Toto hates, as she has three children of her own. To show her anger, as executor of the will, she splits the remaining money between the three siblings, leaving Melissa out of the inheritance.

Even though it isn't Burt's business, he makes his thoughts known to everyone, especially when Toto shows up with her new shiny car. Burt has never been accused of holding back his opinions.

Burt has his own problems; everyone does when it comes to divorce and children. Burt's ex-wife is always making things difficult for his son and stepdaughter's visitations. One weekend, she refuses to return William, claiming she is going on vacation, but it is really just to show her control.

Burt is on the phone with his ex-wife during a party that he and Melissa are attending, and things are not going well. Overhearing the conversation, Toto's sister-in-law comments, "I didn't think anyone could kick Burt's ass, but here we are."

Agitated from the call, Burt snaps, "Stay out of my business, and I won't tell you that your husband is having an affair with a girl in Wendell."

As you can imagine, things get a little crazy for a few minutes, and the party ends abruptly, with most people feeling that Burt is the "asshole." In Burt's defense, Anabel later disassociates herself from drinkers, divorces her cheating husband, and thanks Burt years later, saying, "My life has grown for the better after giving up alcohol."

Chapter 9 – Booze Repair

The next week, Burt takes Melissa to sort out what needs to be done to help her get back on her feet. He pays her fines, clears her bills at the credit bureau, and pays for her SR22 so she can regain insurance. He also asks a friend who is a police officer if they could reconsider her charges for assault, and they do. Burt then speaks with Melissa's boss and asks if he would consider rehiring her if she had a valid driver's license.

"She was great at her job," her boss responds. "I'd be more than happy to have her back."

Melissa returns to work the following week, and they are happy to welcome her. Hopefully, this fresh start will work in her favor. She has a lot of people supporting her — more than most people or spouses have on their journey. Unfortunately, baggage is hard to lose, and not all friends truly have your back, as much as one might think.

The next couple of years go by relatively well, aside from the occasional party where Melissa gets too drunk. Most of the time, it is harmless — just sitting around a campfire while camping, boating, or snowmobiling with friends. However, Melissa never handles hangovers well. Now that age and poor health have begun creeping up on her, everyone pays the price. Every few months, she calls in sick to work due to drinking the night before, putting her job at risk.

The beauty mentioned earlier also starts to work against her. Some colleagues don't appreciate their husbands partying with the "after-hours girls." Women complain to the boss about Melissa flirting with their husbands after work. Eventually, Melissa decides that the hatred she is receiving at work is too much, and she wants to look for another job.

She talks to Burt about it, saying, "The women there just hate me for some reason."

As for Burt, his business, and the boys, things continue to flourish. Burt spends 90% of his time with the boys. Kaden's relationship with his mother starts to decline — not only because of the lack of time they spend together but also due to his growing disrespect for her drinking habits. Any mention of her being intoxicated by a family member leads to her lashing out, viewing it as an attack on her pride.

The boys — especially Kaden, given his close bond with his mother — begin to mimic Melissa when she comes home drunk, causing problems for everyone involved. Burt tries to limit their disrespect, explaining, "It's not helping." But it is tough to manage when he is at work.

Burt usually goes to the gym around 5 PM, while Melissa drinks with her coworkers for a couple of hours most evenings. This distance helps keep tensions lower, as Melissa often passes out when she returns home. However, things continue to deteriorate. Burt hopes that time will heal the wounds that she is harboring.

Melissa's friends support her drinking and partying, and most of them view Burt as "Mr. Goody Two-Shoes." That attitude drives a wedge between Burt and Melissa's married life. They often live in two separate worlds — Burt will not party with her, and she will not recover enough to join him and the boys. Burt focuses on his family, while Melissa focuses on her friends and bar buddies.

Burt knows this arrangement cannot work long-term, but he is willing to endure it until the boys turn eighteen. Once that goal is reached, Burt plans to leave Melissa. For now, he is willing to sacrifice his happiness for his business and the children.

Chapter 10 – Daily Buzz

If the family decides to go snowmobiling, Burt loads the sleds. Melissa will want to stop for beer, causing her to get too intoxicated to ride, or she ends up in the bar with other riders. The biggest problem with Melissa and her addiction is that she never wants to leave at the end of the day, like a lot of drinkers, I guess—party till the cows come home. Many times, the trip will end in fighting with Melissa that it's time to go home, and that the family can't stay till the bar closes just because she wants to.

Sometimes other men intervene to keep a beautiful drunk girl around for the night. Burt will then get branded as the bad guy and kick somebody's ass. Camping is always great for most of the couple's get-togethers for a lot of reasons— it's in the mountains, in a camp, everybody has a spouse, and nobody cares how long the party goes on. Those are good days for the boys and everybody involved. Great memories are made by all attendees, although Melissa isn't an attendee on those hangover days.

Melissa starts doing less with the family to keep Burt from ruining her night, causing Burt to cook dinner for the boys, deal with homework, and do everything a parent should do. Burt has been in a fight with most of Melissa's family and most of her friends. It really creates separation between Burt and Melissa's get-togethers. The boys stick with Burt and have a great relationship with him. Burt gives them attention, plays with them, and allows them to do things most kids their age don't get to.

One time while camping, an intoxicated man gets irritated that the boys are jet skiing in the cove, causing waves and noise that he doesn't want to listen to. The drunk waves them over to the beach, 100 yards from Burt and Melissa's camp. When they oblige and go over to the shore, he grabs them and says, "Get out of the water."

Burt flies down the beach and pounds the guy into the sand, telling the boys, "Go home." Unfortunately, the drunk camper's wife calls the police after the incident. Fortunately, some standby films the whole thing. The cops scold everybody involved, saying, "He better not come back," before leaving. The boys talk about the incident for weeks, discussing everything from them being wrong for causing waves to Burt saving them.

Most of the local bars know the couple—how drunk Melissa will get and how aggressive Burt will get toward men hanging on his wife. Locals stay clear, but newcomers love the affection from a girl dancing, partying, and drinking the night away. Burt knows the cops well, as more than once a bar fight breaks out. Burt is lucky—cops usually arrest drunks over sober people—and Burt is a good talker, having been a bouncer for 10 years. Melissa starts going to house parties to prevent Burt from tracking her down, and sometimes she doesn't make it home at all.

Burt and Melissa aren't the only people or couple bothered by alcohol in their lives. It affects a lot of Americans. Sure, some communities have higher percentages, but it affects millions of humans. One friend of Burt's is struggling himself with drugs and alcohol in his own marriage and talks to Burt about his concerns. His friend says, "I cancelled all my wife's credit cards, but she's still getting drugs delivered somehow without cash."

Burt replies, "I watched a program on TV the other night, and cameras today are high quality with surveillance filming. Maybe that'll help."

Burt's friend takes his advice and installs cameras at his house, both outside and inside the front door. Weeks later,

Burt's friend calls and says, "I'm going to jail because of a jealous rage."

Burt asks, "What happened?"

His friend says, "I found out about an affair with my wife because of the cameras and damaged both her vehicle and the man's vehicle involved in the affair. I even wrote 'your a hore' on her car door."

Laughing, Burt exclaims, "That's not how you spell 'whore' or 'you're!'"

As you can imagine, Burt's friend struggles with an innocent defense in his property damage case.

Chapter 11 – Melissa

One late night, Melissa comes home at 4 o'clock in the morning. She has been partying all night, retreating to somebody's house for the after-party. Burt is in bed and hears her come in the house. He's a light sleeper and knows she's been out again. She goes in the bathroom, still quite intoxicated, and gets ready for bed; Burt sees she isn't wearing undergarments. Burt is pissed but knows it will do no good to accuse her; she'll deny it. So, he just suggests she take a shower. Melissa knows his sarcasm as well as anybody, and that comment sparks her anger. She screams at Burt and goes downstairs to cool off.

Melissa is at a point in her life where alcohol is affecting her in a lot of ways, one of those being blackouts, a medical condition of excessive drinking. The next morning, she remembers nothing of the night before. Burt tells her that it's a bullshit story. Burt has heard of blackouts before; he's been around the block, but he feels it's what people do or say when they go home with an ugly person. Burt has been crazy drunk before but can remember everything to a T before passing out; but that's not always the case with alcoholics. As time goes on, Burt realizes alcoholics really do function for hours even though their brain isn't at full function, especially reasoning.

A few weeks later, Burt fixes dinner for the family while the boys do their homework, waiting for Melissa to get home from work. Melissa doesn't show and never answers the phone for Burt's calls when the party starts, so Burt and the boys eat as it's getting late.

Burt starts to wash the dishes and hears a car pull up. A few minutes later, Melissa staggers in the front door. She states she got too drunk to drive, so a friend brought her home. Burt asks who that was. Melissa won't say, and Burt continues to ask questions, each question getting more personal, making Melissa angrier with each line.

Suddenly, she punches Burt in the face while he's still washing the dishes. He quickly restrains her from hitting him again, all brought on by guilty pride. She screams bloody murder, calling Burt every name in the book, causing the neighbors to call the cops. When the boys ask the two of them to stop fighting, Melissa goes into the bedroom; just before the cops show up. Burt is just finishing the dishes when there is a knock on the door, it's the police, the boys are ready for bed and sitting in the kitchen. Burt answers the door, and the police ask what is going on; Burt not wanting any problem as it always costs him money, says nothing. The police tell him that the neighbors dialed 911, so something must be happening, and Burt invites them inside to calm them down.

Burt asks Kaden to grab his mom while the police question him and William. They wait until Melissa and Kaden return, once everyone is present, the police question them all in the room.

Afterward, the police ask one last question, "How come there is blood in your mustache?"

Burt hadn't noticed that his nose is bleeding into his beard.

Melissa is arrested and placed in the police car. Once again, all this drinking will cost Burt money and result in Melissa spending another night in jail. Melissa was given a 72-hour restraining order, so she slept at her sister's house for a few days, with both Melissa and Toto venting their frustration about Burt.

Time heals all wounds, and just a few weeks go by before one of the relatives throws a birthday party for the nieces. Burt probably wouldn't attend, given how upset Toto is with Burt and Melissa's marriage problems, but Burt's nieces love him, and he has promised they can spend the night at Aunt and Uncle Burt's house.

Burt and Melissa drive separately, so Burt loads up the girls and leaves for home. Melissa will be right behind him. Once home, he gets everyone in bed and watches TV in the bedroom for a while until he gets tired and turns off the TV.

Before he falls asleep, he hears Melissa pull into the driveway, although an extra vehicle pulls in with her. Burt listens and recognizes the voice of a friend of theirs, but he doesn't really care at the moment. A friend, right?

The bedroom door is partially open when Melissa comes to the door and closes it tight, thinking Burt is asleep. Burt waits a few minutes and gets out of bed, quietly opening the door to listen to what's going on, standing in the dark.

It's funny what people think, or don't think, while intoxicated, that drives them to come into a house with children, guns, and Burt. Nevertheless, things are gravitating toward sex.

Burt goes back into the bedroom, pulls out his .45, and heads back toward the living room, turning on a light as he approaches the couch where both are intertwined in the act. Byron freaks out when the light comes on, realizing he's been caught, but he's not as surprised as he is staring into the barrel of a Colt .45.

Burt orders Byron to hit the road, which he does immediately, leaving some clothes and his shoes behind. It's the first time Burt truly believes in her infidelity, mainly because it's the only time he witnesses it. He really doesn't want to accept it, but at this moment, it is what it is.

Burt struggles with the reality of it, anger boiling inside him. He knows that if he stays, something bad will happen. He knows the boys need him around for at least a few more years.

He loads some of his guns and leaves the house in the middle of the night, deciding to travel to a hunting area he loves. Burt reaches the hunting area just as the sun begins to rise, but his plan to kill some animals diminishes as those are the things he loves most from childhood.

He sets up on a ridgetop for an hour or so, then drives back to the valley. When he arrives home, Toto is in his bedroom, where Melissa is trying to sleep off a hangover. Toto scolds Melissa about her actions, saying that everyone in the valley has heard about Melissa and Byron's act.

Not only is Toto upset that it ruins the family name, but she's also furious about the disrespect Melissa shows with Toto's daughters in the house at the time of the affair. It's a very hard act for Melissa to sweep under the rug, both for herself and for her good friend's husband—one that never gets buried, even to this day.

Melissa would never expose herself in public; she is quite conservative. Burt recalls one time when she wears a blouse and her uncle comments on how big her breasts are. Melissa goes off on him, asking him to leave the house at that moment. Burt's reaction is just to think about how many family members in society would ever make that comment; it seems kind of perverted to him.

At no point would she attend a function, bar, or otherwise, dressed like a call girl, showing any skin. But as the song goes, "Tequila Makes Her Clothes Fall Off," she sometimes comes home with less. Any man who approaches her in an aggressive sexual manner is instantly sent on his way. But three drinks later, she's a different girl.

Friends who don't know her very well might think she drinks a lot, but she can actually drink very little. That is part of the problem she faces. She never drinks hard liquor, only beer. After 3-4 drinks, she's slurring her words; after 4-5, she's hanging on people, and after 6, she's passing out. Her tolerance for alcohol is quite low.

The real issue is her addiction. After just one beer, she isn't leaving the bar until she's passing out. Blacking out is real for her, and when it happens, she never believes anyone about her actions from the night before. No one—not even her best friends—can convince her of the reality. Somehow, Melissa is able to store those memories away with other parts of her life, and no matter how impossible it seems, it is.

Melissa's brain, like that of all severe alcoholics, uses primal functions for flight or fight, resulting in difficult relationship conversations.

Melissa is not an aggressive person, and those who know her well, like Burt, don't even think she likes fighting. She just strikes out when intoxicated due to a primal brain response. Melissa carries a lot of baggage because of alcohol, and sometimes that baggage catches up with you.

One evening in the saloon, Melissa walks in for a drink. A woman who has been drinking for a while approaches her, angry and loud. She has unfinished business with Melissa from a past husband problem. Perhaps Melissa has slept with her ex-husband, but whatever the reason, the woman is aggressive, twice the size of Melissa, and wearing a western getup with boots and a skirt.

Melissa wants nothing to do with this situation, but before she can escape, the woman grabs her and throws her on the floor, jumping onto her chest and trying to punch her in the head. Great fear washes over Melissa; she feels a chance she might die. At best, she hasn't been beaten this badly because this girl is playing for keeps.

The girl rides high on Melissa's chest, and in a panic, Melissa bites her between the panties and her thigh—the only thing she knows to do in that moment of fear. She bites hard, fighting for her life. It's the only way she feels she can fight back, as she lies on her back, her arms pinned, taking punches to the face.

Within a second of biting down on this woman's crotch, it's like lightning strikes her; the girl freezes in a spread-eagle position until Melissa releases her grip. At that point, the girl recoils into a fetal position, covering the spot, blood and all.

Burt is no doctor but feels that this area might be a tender section. The fight is over, and so is the party.

One evening, while most of the couples are still talking and enjoying each other's company, Burt has purchased a Tyson fight on his home theater HBO and invited the boys over to watch. Melissa and the other wives decide to make it a girls' night out; the boys watch the fight while the girls go to the bar. Burt thinks it's stupid but loves boxing, so he shrugs it off.

The fight goes late into the night, and just when it's about to finish, Melissa comes home, very intoxicated, while the other girls stay out on the town drinking. Melissa greets everyone and announces she is going to bed, then retreats to the bedroom.

During the last round of the fight, she re-enters the TV room wearing only a smile and asks Burt when he is coming to bed. Burt jumps up and escorts her back to the bedroom, tucking her in. The Tyson fight wraps up, and the guests, trying not to act like they just witnessed something bizarre, head home. Burt's mind wanders, thinking about the memories of a knockout — Iron Mike or his naked wife.

Even when you think alcohol couldn't affect the day, it can always rear its ugly head. On a weekend snowmobiling trip at 4th of July Creek, when most people are just trying to survive the long day filled with hill climbs and the extreme agility required to avoid freezing to death if something goes wrong, Melissa still manages to get into trouble.

Smiley Creek in winter can be beautiful but also extremely cold, with temperatures well below freezing. This is one of those days. When Burt, the boys, and Melissa pull into the parking lot, the temperature is minus 32 degrees Fahrenheit. It's so cold that all members of the group have to put their sleds in Burt's trailer to warm up for a while before they can start.

The group heads out for the bowls of 4th of July Creek on a beautiful sunny day. The snow is great, making for a wonderful outing—except Melissa is getting intoxicated. The winters of Idaho don't offer much sunlight, and the temperature drops extremely fast at that time of year; you'd best get out during daylight hours if you know what's good for you.

As the group starts the long ride out, the sun edges toward the horizon, darkness creeping in along with subzero temperatures. They reach a bridge to cross the river, slowing down to maneuver in single file. Melissa, and only Melissa, thinks the river is the best way to cross, even as darkness approaches. Burt stops when Melissa's sled stalls in the deep water of the river. Smart enough to stand on her fuel tank and hood, Melissa cries out, and Burt can't believe it.

While most of the group finds it funny, Burt and a few of his close friends see it as dangerous. They're still eight miles from the parking lot, and a human is now in icy water. Burt and his friend, Gelski, pull tow straps from their sleds while Melissa screams that her sled is sinking. Without help, she believes she will die shortly.

Burt wades into the river, carrying Melissa out of danger to the bank, with only one of her feet getting wet. He then takes the tow strap back to hook it onto the skis of Melissa's sled. Burt's friends try to pull the sled out, but it won't budge, frozen in place. Leaving the sled would surely be the demise of a $9,000 purchase.

Burt attempts to lift the sled, standing in chest-deep 31-degree water, but can't exert any force without using his legs. He must squat to lift the 300-pound sled out of the icy water. Now completely wet, Burt manages to get the sled on the bank, but it won't start since the engine is full of water. He asks his friend for help to tow it back to the parking lot.

Melissa rides Burt's snowmobile as Gelski tows Burt back on the eight-mile journey. At 60 mph, the wind chill is 50 degrees below zero, and Burt is slipping into hypothermia by the time he's towed into the parking lot. Burt knows the conditions of hypothermia well; he strips off his wet clothes and walks naked into the restaurant. The owner recognizes the dire emergency and grabs blankets and coffee for Burt before he goes into shock.

Melissa is lucky, but Burt is even luckier. Once again, because of Melissa's choices, the dangers of alcohol affect more than just the drinker.

Chapter 12 – Boys will be Boys

The boys are old enough to do most adult things now: work, play, snowmobile—any activity that Burt usually does. Young boys this age enjoy activities like this and eat it up most of the time. They start attending the gym, working out as boys big enough to ride their own snowmobile, ATV, and any toy available. Kaden has always liked hunting and has a passion toward guns and ammo, so he starts helping with reloading as Burt shoots many rounds at the gun range each week. In late summer, early fall, Burt and his hunting friends go to the shooting range almost every evening and shoot till dark. Kaden really starts to excel in learning ballistics, gun actions, and calibers. Even though Kaden doesn't do well in school and struggles with ADHD, he memorizes every grain of powder, bullet type, and sight design. His commitment to exact detail and attention almost counteracts his learning diagnosis and creates something he hadn't felt in life: success. Both boys go snowmobiling, camping, and working as adults, with no concern about Melissa, but Burt is really bothered that his wife isn't in the picture most of the time.

Burt focuses on the boys; even though it's not the way he wants it, Melissa is something he can't control, so he focuses on what he can control: memories with the boys. Sometimes they go three to four days each week without even seeing Melissa, and, as life would have it, they get farther from her. Burt loves the outdoors, so that's where they are a lot of the time. They hike to lakes, go camping, ATV rides, and hunting trips, all of which Kaden loves, though some are not William's favorites. William is good in school, loves his laptop, loves movies, and reading; Kaden is pretty much the opposite of that. Burt tries to treat them the same, but it's difficult with kids, especially kids who are polar opposites. William loves scientific movies like *Twister*, while Kaden likes hunting movies like *Rambo*. Burt jokes around with people that when he sees the high school principal come up on caller ID, he knows either William is getting an achievement award or Kaden is getting reprimanded for fighting. Any chance to go hike or hunt, Kaden is excited; if it's swimming or IMAX, William is excited. Through it all, they are brothers, and, when push comes to shove, they have each other's back.

Some of the struggles Kaden has are with his ADHD learning; he does well with Burt as Burt is an ex-teacher and understands his condition. Kaden is constantly asking questions, mostly scenarios that even the best of priests couldn't answer. Luckily, Burt enjoys teaching and talking, so it doesn't bother him too much, but others in the vehicle will be insane by trip's end. Opposite to education, Kaden has a great desire to learn about guns and hunting, snowmobile racing, and, because of it, puts an immense amount of thought and time into it. Burt buys him racing sleds, allows him use of guns, gear to hunt. Kaden enjoys hanging with his grandfather when he can, though that slowly gets less as Kaden grows older and able to hang with older hunters. At one time, William and Kaden get in a fight about something, and William punches Kaden in the throat, which seems to bring the fight to an end. Burt tells each of them to knock off the pestering, arguing, and act like brothers, while Melissa wants William reprimanded for throat punching. Melissa isn't satisfied, as she feels throat punching is beyond "just brothers fighting," at which Burt disagrees. Burt recalls one trip they went on, where Kaden and William were in the hotel swimming pool, and most of the people left in a few short minutes after the boys got in the pool. After a few minutes, Burt realizes Kaden has his probation ankle bracelet on, and parents get their kids out of the pool for safety, allowing the boys to have the pool to themselves.

Burt spends numerous hours preparing and scouting for hunting game in the fall; be it birds, deer, antelope, or elk—the biggest concern is elk. Burt may spend that time reloading, shooting, scouting, or glassing for animals; sometimes it requires scouting four to five hours away or spending the weekend in the gun room, reloading and adjusting. One weekend, Burt and Darin are working on reloading ammo in the gun room and leave to grab a bite to eat in the kitchen, at which time they hear a noise. Burt heads to the gun room only to find Kaden placing a gun back in the case, acting as though nothing happened. Burt scolds him not to touch any gun until he's around. Later, Darin discovers the scope was bent from the fall, costing $1,400 and the time to recalibrate. Burt is furious and tells Kaden he isn't allowed to go with them that weekend to scout for elk. Kaden is devastated. It is a good learning experience and gives Melissa a chance to hang with Kaden for the weekend.

One hunt that a lot of Burt's friends draw tags for is exceptionally fun for Kaden; one he tells his mother is the greatest weekend of his life after he returns home—a hunt of a lifetime. A week of antelope hunting, a week of deer, and a week of elk—three weeks of nothing but wilderness. Kaden has a great opportunity for these types of things; Burt gives him opportunities to hunt and shoot, and Kaden receives guns and optics few people ever get the chance to use. Burt gets him within 150 yards of a standing antelope, 400 yards from an elk, and Kaden shoots a deer on his own morning hunt. Burt and his other hunting buddies also get animals; it is a great year. Kaden is in his element, not only with seasoned hunters but with an abundance of animals. Kaden loves the excitement of each kill, sometimes being right there as a part of it and sometimes riding up with his ATV. After that trip, the group knows him as "the gutter" because of his interest in caring for the butchering of the animals—a badge that Kaden accepts with honor.

The next year, Kaden, Burt, and Darin go alone, as no other group hunter draws a tag besides Kaden for elk. They go on a shorter trip that year with fewer tags, as Burt is busy at work. William doesn't want to go hunting because of school and his debate training for state competition, and Burt doesn't want to leave William at home alone with Melissa for very long. They arrive just the night before opening day with little time to prepare for the hunt, getting up early with hopes of getting an animal first thing. Right at daybreak, about halfway up to the tree line, Burt, Kaden, and Darin run into some other hunters on horseback, and the day starts off with aggression. Walkers don't like horsemen, horsemen don't like ATVs—the list goes on for everyone on the mountain, and today is no different. Burt gets off his ATV to open a gate for the hunters, both his group and the two men on horseback, which starts the argument. Burt tells the riders to ride through, saying he'll close the gate for them, but the horsemen respond that they can close the gate themselves, as they want distance from motor vehicles. Burt shrugs, saying, "OK," and rides on. The horse bucks the rider off, running toward Burt, who jumps off the ATV and catches the horse, returning it downhill to the owner. The horsemen, unaware of Burt's thousands of hours in the saddle, assume he only rides ATVs because of his kids. The groups exchange heated words but eventually go their separate ways. Burt decides to let the horsemen take the ridgeline along the trees— it's a good game trail. Burt exclaims to Darin that if they sit tight in the rock cliffs, perhaps the elk will circle around once they hear the horses. They climb into the rocks, parking ATVs below in the brush, and find a spot where they can see the ridge. Burt has Kaden sit next to him so he can keep him quiet and direct his shot. They sit for an hour or so, and Burt spots a cow elk 600 yards away, hoping it fades westward, allowing them to make a shot on a bull in the herd. Slowly, the herd appears, and there's a bull. The entire herd walks within 100 yards of the rocks, and Burt tells Kaden to shoot the bull in the front shoulder, as the terrain is steep and they can't let the animal run downhill into the trees. Kaden shoots, and the bull drops only 15 feet away. Burt, fearing they might be spotted by the horsemen, quickly instructs everyone to move. They gut, skin, and load the animal, taking it to the meat packer later that day.

They pack up the next day, and Kaden is eager to show everyone in town the elk he harvested, admiring Burt for his call to sit in the rocks.

William is a little different with hunting; he loves the outdoors but isn't interested in the hunt itself. William draws for animals sometimes and goes along, but he isn't focused on filling his tag. Many times, Burt and William belly-crawl for hundreds of feet to make a shot, yet William doesn't take it. Burt respects this, as hunting isn't just about the kill—it's about the experience. However, Kaden feels beside himself on those hunts.

Burt has Kaden and William compete in wrestling, something he had done in high school, because he believes sports help young kids succeed and improve as adults. William doesn't enjoy it as much; he doesn't like non-academic competitions, but Kaden loves it. Burt would take them to competitions across the state, where Kaden would do quite well; William would usually do well for a couple of rounds and then be done. Kaden wins a couple of tournaments, where he's excited because neither boy has much training like other contestants. Melissa would attend most of them; with Burt's help, he would pour her into the truck, her still looming from a hangover at 5:00 AM. On one occasion, she sleeps in the truck until 2:00 PM. Kaden wins first in the tourney, and she doesn't wake up till they're back at the truck. Kaden isn't happy with his mom, and he makes it known for the rest of the day, at dinner, and the long drive home. Perhaps pride, guilt, something would drive Melissa to never apologize, but instead, she gets angry at all involved, not making the situation any better. As tough as Kaden is, Burt laughs at one meet in Challis because he's in a weight class with a girl wrestler—a young Native American girl that's tough as nails. Burt and the boys have seen her wrestle other boys at other tournaments, crushing the pride of the boys they beat, some boys refusing to ever wrestle again. Luckily at that tournament, the young girl gets eliminated before Kaden has to wrestle her. Kaden often wrestles without his gear, as his ADHD would cause him to forget it during departure, sometimes looking quite foolish in just shorts and socks.

Kaden's ADHD creates problems in his ability to get along, comingle, and adjust to what people expect of him. Some are harmless, some low-cost, but other times drive a wedge with those who surround him. Forgetting things is just a normal day for Kaden, and Burt scolds him on many occasions for not paying attention. People use the phrase "he would lose his head if it wasn't tied on" jokingly, I think, but Kaden really lives by that. Perhaps that's a big problem with his mom; perhaps she suffers as well from ADHD, and alcohol just amplifies it. It's something America struggles with, diagnosing young kids before life engulfs them. Burt would always say parents with children diagnosed with ADHD don't know what the real definition is. He'll tell them, "Hang with Kaden for a week, and he'll change your mind." Burt tries to let Kaden do things on his own, as he feels Kaden needs that to mature into an adult. It seems Melissa never pays much of the price for her child; Burt feeds, clothes, entertains, and replaces Kaden's daily misforgivings.

Scouting is always a fun time of the year; it's been all winter and summer, and it isn't serious for a harvest. Burt usually films a lot of it because noise isn't going to make or break a hunt. Practicing glassing, calling, tracking — all things to make a hunter a better guide, to help one another during the actual hunt. Hunting alone is dangerous and shouldn't normally be done because of things that can happen, even with today's technology. Scouting is different, as no large animal is going to be harvested; most participants aren't armed, and the weather is quite nice. On one trip in the Herd Lake region, they all split up after riding to the area of the hunt. Burt explains that everybody will meet back there at 3 PM, and they all ride off on ATVs. Kaden is eager to be on his own; Burt has always babysat him for protection, but now it's time to try the skills he's learned. They all have a good day and meet back at 3 PM at the designated spot, except for Kaden. The group waits for him. About an hour later, Kaden comes riding up, saying he's sorry for being late but was tracking a large bull. Burt tells Kaden that's not how a hunting group does it and asks where his binoculars are. Kaden looks confused, then says he doesn't know. Kaden explains he thinks he set them on a hillside and then must have driven off without them. Burt also notices that Kaden's feet and pant legs are wet. Burt asks about the waterlogged look. Again, Kaden knows the answer, yet can't escape the guilt, and replies, "Wet feet are dead feet!" The group backtracks for a little way, and then Burt calls off the search, leaving his $350 binoculars to blend into mother earth. At times, Burt feels bad about chewing on Kaden's ass so much for his mistakes, even confiding in one of his friends for advice. Burt asks Gelski if he thinks he's a born asshole or just needs to let it slide more often. Gelski's response is, "Dude, I don't know how you do it, every day!"

On a weekend bird hunting trip, Burt and Kaden are walking a field for grouse when a group of grouse starts running along a ditch, which drains to the gravel forest service road. Kaden runs after them, and they all fly when Kaden gets close. Kaden, being young, doesn't think and shoots toward the road. A mountain biker freaks out and pedals toward Kaden, screaming bloody murder; by the time Burt gets there, the man is punching Kaden in the chest, pushing him back with each punch. The biker is with his very young son as well, so Burt doesn't beat the man unconscious when he reaches the scene. Instead, he tells the guy to back off. The guy realizes he's bitten off more than he can chew and later calls the police. The forest ranger gives Kaden a ticket for shooting next to a highway, the ranger not really understanding Kaden is a minor. The ticket then goes to Burt, as he's the guardian in charge. Although this doesn't bother Burt much; he's not applying for a job anytime soon. Nevertheless, Burt pays the ticket; it's a misdemeanor for "shooting from a highway."

Kaden, from a very young age, has been on a snowmobile, probably since he was 5 or 6 years old. He started out by riding in front of Burt, who would ride all day with him hanging onto the handlebar, later riding his own. Occasionally, he'd ride his mom's sled, and Melissa would ride with Burt if beers had their say. Melissa is strong, tough, awry, and a good snowmobiler; she goes on a lot of rides early on without alcohol, and Burt enjoys those days because she seldom whines about the rides being tough. On a trip up Hedemann late one spring, the group goes up a climb to take them way into the backcountry; once in, you must come back. On the way back, just before the easy cat track home, there's a hill climb that everyone struggles to reach the top. Burt is helping sledders up the climb, including Melissa, when suddenly she decides to go out another way and speeds downhill through an avalanche chute. Burt freaks, knowing there is no other way. He screams at Platts to help him, knowing the chute is very dangerous. They follow her tracks to where they see her sled and know why she stopped; both shut their sleds down 50 feet from the edge. Melissa's sled is 3 feet from going over a 200-foot cliff; she's very lucky. Burt tells her to never do that again, no matter how angry she is, and she agrees. Burt and Platts pull the sled backward until they can turn it around to face uphill. Burt instructs Melissa to take his sled and go to the rest of the group up the long hill climb; his sled is built for those climbs. Burt rides hers up to the top, as he's been riding sleds forever and has learned techniques to help him on any sled; he wishes Melissa would learn patience as one of her techniques. Maybe Burt caused some of the drinking, so Melissa had some liquid courage to ride. She seemed crazy, but deep down, maybe she didn't really like rides the group of friends enjoyed. Burt admits to friends that he doesn't play friendly to some sports; he gets bored from riding without danger, and perhaps Melissa gets bored from not drinking.

Kaden doesn't have the experience at a young age, but fear doesn't bother him in the least; he'll go at most things with the desire to conquer. He's always been fighting with older kids, so bigger challenges don't affect him like most; this is a great attribute and a great curse. He's good at snowmobiling and really likes going with Burt and his guy friends; they go places that challenge his ability. Burt usually gets him a new sled because of racing, wrecking, or just for a better model. Burt loves Yamaha and wants to prove a point. Yamahas aren't sold in large quantities in the West, mainly because of weight, but Burt loves their engines. Most of his sleds are altered from factory condition, some NOX injected, but Kaden loves the fact that he can outrun any of his friends most of the time. Once, riding up Baker Creek Lake, Burt and Kaden go by themselves for a quick outing for the day. It had snowed 2 feet, and Burt loves freshie with his sleds, so they just take the 2 highly modified sleds. Once reaching the lake, a group of dozens of riders is parked on the lake, as it's too deep for most sleds to maneuver, and they don't want to get stuck. Burt and Kaden play around a little right by the lake to feel things out, and then Burt starts to climb the huge avalanche chute above the lake. He goes about a fourth of the way to see if the snow feels safe and comes back down, while Kaden goes until he gets stuck in the steep part of the chute. Burt freaks because of the probability of an avalanche. He has to ride up and help Kaden get his sled out. Burt goes off on Kaden as this is the way people die in avalanches, telling him to never do that again, continuing to look uphill to watch for a slide until freeing Kaden. Burt then shoots his turbo-charged sled to the top, and they go home for the day, not before getting a thumbs-up from the group on the frozen lake. The next day, one of Burt's friends dies in an avalanche in the same area; it brings a chilling reminder of death from mother earth.

Those 3–4 years when the marriage was good, the snow was excellent lent to some great times with friends snowmobiling to some of the highest peaks in Idaho. Something few people

52

enjoy at any time in their lives, and those kinds of experiences would certainly make life worth living. Living life close to the edge results in problems sometimes unforeseen, no matter the precaution. On one outing by Galena Summit, the group is riding up in headwater and descending a steep hill, but manageable even by novice riders. The group all descends to a flat spot where Burt and Platts are climbing a short chute across a creek until Burt sees Melissa stuck halfway up the hill everyone just came down. Burt is a little surprised and rides back up the hill toward Melissa and parks beside her, asking what happened. She responds that she ran over a little pine tree, which stopped her sled, causing her to fall off. Burt tells her to take his sled down, and he'll get her sled off the sapling and meet her on the flat. Melissa agrees. Burt dislodges the sled, goes to the bottom, and asks if she's okay. Melissa responds she thinks she hit her head on the ski because she feels weird, like she's drunk. Burt looks at her eyes and tells the group he needs to call it a day and go back to the parking lot. Burt asks Melissa if she can ride her sled, and she says she doesn't know the way and is kind of dizzy. So he asks Platts to ride to the top and pick him up. Putting Melissa in front of him on his sled, he takes her to the top of the mountain where the cat track is. Melissa states she can drive the groomed trail if she can follow someone else, as the cat track is flat and freshly groomed all the way to the parking lot. Burt then gets a ride back down with Platts to retrieve the other sled. They all ride single file to the bottom of the range. Melissa is doing just fine riding behind a friend and makes the trip down. By the time the group reaches the parking lot, about an hour later, Melissa doesn't really know what's going on. Burt feels she might just be cold, so he suggests they go into the restaurant to get something to eat. Burt orders her some coffee and asks the waitress for a warm blanket, which is common in Stanley Basin. Melissa is getting worse by this time, asking the same question repeatedly. Burt loads her up in the truck and heads for the hospital — it's the longest drive of his life. Once they reach the hospital and Melissa is admitted, the doctor determines she has a concussion, deciding to keep her overnight for observation. The next day, she has a mild headache but feels much better and is able to go to work in a few days. There's a buzz of people who feel Melissa wasn't wearing a helmet, was going too fast, and probably those who feel Burt is at fault.

Chapter 13 – Burt

Burt is different from most people he knows, or most of the people around him anyway! He takes a bullet for those he loves but cares less about most others, and that's what makes non-friends dislike him. His close friends all know that, but Melissa can't understand why it is so important to her, and she probably never will. Burt doesn't like people or large gatherings, which is why he enjoys the outdoors and the kids in his life. Burt understands that this is a problem between him and a lot of people, and a wedge between him and Melissa. Burt likes kids enough to go to dinner with the boys and his nieces just to give them a night out. Toto doesn't like the situation, but the girls really enjoy it, even if it's just for ice cream.

At one restaurant, one of the nieces eats a spoonful of hot mustard, almost choking on the heat. After gaining composure, she states, "We have much to learn from the Chinese."

At one time, Burt and the kids go out every couple of weeks, but as time goes on, Toto puts a stop to it.

Even though Melissa only hears, "My way or the highway," Burt protects her at any cost, an undying Viking pact. It's something an addict doesn't understand because, for most of them, they would sell anybody for a beer, and it's something her friends and coworkers don't comprehend. At one point, Burt asks Melissa about him or beer; she chooses beer, and he knows that answer determines she is a hopeless alcoholic.

Burt loves to snowmobile, sometimes with just some guys, but mostly with family. It is a skill he likes and involves being in nature. One of the reasons Burt loves snowmobiling so much is that it is a sport that changes every day—every snowfall, every different machine. No other sport offers that as well. Burt owns boats, jet skis, has waterskied, and plays different sports, but being in mother nature, a wintery paradise, takes high skill and a healthy body to make it to places others can't reach. At high altitude and working 400-500 pounds around the trees, rocks, and creeks, it takes most smokers, drinkers, and out-of-shape people out of the picture, which Burt enjoys being away from. Most snowmobilers use the groomed trails, and out West, they are only used to run from hill to hill, while back East, they go from town to town.

Melissa doesn't like the gym, so she has a hard time going to intense areas, but Burt, however, loves the gym and keeps his body in shape to enable just that. Working, snowmobiling, hiking, and hunting all require staying in good shape. Burt has been in gyms since he was a teenager. Melissa goes on occasion, like when her brother comes to stay for two weeks while he is on leave from the Air Force. Melissa's brother goes each evening with Burt, and Melissa tags along and tries to pretend she enjoys it. Burt gets along very well with Melissa's brother; they always have fun joking around with each other. Burt tells Melissa's brother, "It's good that Flyboys don't have to be strong."

Melissa has a hard time, probably because of her childhood, differentiating between drinkers and real friends, as with a lot of humans. Real friends may have differences and fight occasionally but will never stab you in the back, ever. Drinking buddies won't and can't keep from focusing on a high rather than what's right. Melissa finds out but never really learns, and it's hard to say goodbye to any friend. Burt has some close friends; none of them drink except one. Melissa has one older woman, but as far as friends her age, all are alcoholics and have problems with everything from health to police and their relationships. It is not good for the protection of each other's friends, and inebriation makes for poor choices at a time of need late at night. Once the girls start partying, they never worry about each other, and it's not just Melissa's group—this is true for most groups of intoxicated girls. Melissa gets drinking, and not one of her friends watches her back or keeps her actions as straight and narrow as possible. Not one of the girls reacts to anything that the other is doing while drinking together or partying in the bar, even though it is the right thing to do.

Burt has tried to have discussions with the girls when time allows to chat during camping, snowmobiling, and other activities that Melissa might be absent at the time. Melissa has two sets of standards she lives by: one is sober daytime Melissa, while the other is party-all-night Melissa. Which one is correct? Burt tries to suggest that the pre-beer human is the correct one, or they wouldn't have commercials about taking away a drunk man's car keys. Once, a friend of both Burt and Melissa, a woman, asks Burt, "Do you think you are better than me because I drink?" With that kind of ridiculous question, Burt answers, "Yes!"

Melissa's drinking is never half-assed; being an alcoholic, she drinks until she passes out every night she drinks. Sometimes she doesn't have her keys to get in the house, usually because someone drives her home, and she doesn't have her truck keys either. She has lost so many keys in her life that she leaves keys in her truck's ignition and only carries her key fob in her bra. No truck, no house keys, and that costs her to sleep on the doorstep more than once. Burt wonders how many people drive by to see a woman sleeping on the doormat like an Amazon package. Her blackouts become worse as she continues to drink, even though she doesn't believe things that she might have done, as her friends tell her the next day. One evening, while the bar hosts a karaoke contest that is being recorded in a downtown bar, Melissa decides to enter while she is drinking excessively during the night. Her singing continues to get worse as the evening goes on, but by evening's end, she is just lying on the stage floor, murmuring the words. Luckily, almost everybody in the bar knows her and just laughs it off as Burt carries her off.

Like most addictions, they continue to get worse as time goes on. The girls have it tougher than men, mainly because of their size, but most of the girls attend the bar with their

57

husbands, so they go home when they leave as a couple. That is tough for Burt as he can't just take off at 5:00 sharp to meet up with drinking couples. If Burt comes to the bar at 7-8 o'clock to pick up Melissa, she has a tizzy fit about getting in a truck for the night. If that is the case, this story wouldn't have been written. Each night seems to get worse for intoxication to incidents, resulting from fighting to death. One late weekend night, the group parties till the bar shuts down, with no one thinking to take care of the other. This results in one of the girlfriend's brothers dying in a car wreck as he leaves the bar. Being an educator for many years and knowing the trials of teaching, Burt finds that tragedy doesn't affect the minds of humans very often. It is a sad fact, but it is true. The party continues a week later.

Again, life can deal cards not wanted, and lo and behold, Melissa gets another DUI on the way home from the bar one evening. She has had a good run, perhaps five years since her last one, and in one way, Melissa thinks she has some sort of guardian angel. This time, Burt's business is thriving, and he has over 20 employees driving about 10 vehicles. Burt's insurance company calls and explains she cannot drive any company vehicles, leaving Melissa on foot again. What is a husband to do? What is a business owner to do? What is a friend to do? Burt is at a crossroads. Burt talks to Melissa and tries to explain to her and see his side of the story, although Melissa wants nothing to do with it. Burt puts his foot down and makes his choice: they will split up, leaving Melissa without a home, vehicle, and phone, all of which she has never paid for, let alone thought about what it means to pay for them. Melissa is furious, reacting like never before, perhaps going from the top to the bottom in life; she is beyond scorned. Melissa storms out of the house and goes to her friends' house. She calls Burt later, perhaps she is scared Burt will call the cops, as this is quite rare for her to accommodate Burt's feelings with a courtesy call.

The next day, I'm sure Melissa thinks it is just another day. Burt goes by her place of work to grab the pickup truck she has been driving. He has the spare keys; Melissa doesn't know Burt is planning this, and even her phone is inside the truck as the battery is dead from not charging all night. Funny as it may seem, Melissa doesn't notice she has lost her vehicle and phone until about 7:00 p.m. because she has gone to have drinks with girlfriends and wash her sorrows away. Melissa borrows her friends' phone and calls Burt to see if he has it. He responds, "Yes, and you won't get any of it back due to your legal problems."

She goes ballistic and calls the police. They explain the truck and phone are in the business name, so she has no legal authority to get them returned. Melissa does what she has been taught as a young girl: survive at any cost by building resentment, walls, and surrounding herself with like-minded friends.

Burt goes about his life as always, with too much going on in his day-to-day schedule to focus on love when everything from work, kids, and friends takes up 18 hours. Melissa is living with a friend of hers, gets by without a cell phone, and parties like a rock star. Her life is back to where it was a decade earlier, and believe it or not, she is quite comfortable; there is something to be said about complacency. Toto has had to spend a lot of time with her immediate family over the last few years and has been employed like most couples in today's economy. Melissa and Toto miss each other's company, so they start to hang out. It gives them time to regress, and it gives Melissa a mode of transportation. Given Toto's hatred towards Burt and her ability to accept drinkers, the two devise a plan. Toto works for the prosecutor at the city, and she suggests Melissa file for a divorce and take custody of Kaden as it must be done and will teach Burt a lesson. Both Melissa and Toto have told the attorney how asinine and unreasonable Burt is, a trick of the trade they have both learned as younger girls. The girls, Melissa and Toto, stop by with the cops to retrieve Kaden and his belongings. He doesn't want to go with his mom, but Burt tells him to go for now because it is legal, and after a couple of weeks, it will be over. Kaden usually stops by the house to see Burt and William every day or so on his way home to his mom's place of residence. This goes on for a few months, but Kaden is not happy with the situation, and his mom knows it, which makes her feel alone and afraid.

Chapter 14 – Kaden

Kaden turns sixteen, and he is excited about it. Burt tells him to stop by the house, which he does, and discovers that Burt is giving him an ATV so that he has some mode of transportation. This allows him to come over every day if he desires, go fishing, or at least take his dog for a ride to play in the river. Kaden loves that gift and can tell it's Burt's way of expressing he wants him around, even if his aunt and mother do not. Kaden knows his fun activities have always included Burt. Melissa perhaps feels it's something her father would do; she purchases Kaden a twelve-pack of beer, thinking it would push him away from Burt but also bring them closer. It's a thought that is illegal for a reason and morally ridiculous, but Burt has no control over the situation. Kaleb is young and gullible, so he drinks the beer with some friends and proceeds to go to a dance at the high school. He is arrested at the school dance for being intoxicated and is placed in a police car, where he continues his rant. While his hands are cuffed in the back seat and the police arrest one of his friends, Kaden kicks the roof and windows of the police cruiser, causing a lot of damage to the car. The officers call Burt as it's the only number they have for a contact since he is a minor. It's a reminder that Kaden is following a road not unlike his family history, which Burt doesn't like.

Kaden receives a ticket for minor consumption and is required to fix the damages to the police car. Burt has one of his friends replace the broken windows on the car; the police let other small damages slide through the cracks of police work. The juvenile judge tells Kaden that he is on probation and if he does well in school, this thing can go away, but if not, he will be sent to Twin Falls to the juvenile detention center. Toto is disgusted with Melissa for embarrassing her at work with her relationship with a nephew, as she has to hear about it for two days. Kaden is expelled from school for five days as a penalty for being intoxicated on school grounds. During that week,

Kaden runs all over the valley, hanging with other kids who have been kicked out or have dropped out of school. Kaden becomes "the man" for breaking out the police car windows to his new friends and feels at home with drinking and smoking cigarettes with his new group. A few weeks later, he stops by to talk to William and see what he's been doing, as he hasn't talked to him due to his absence from school. Before he goes inside the house, he goes around back to smoke a cigarette, throwing the butt in the dry weeds behind the garage, and it catches the house on fire. William calls Burt, saying that the back of the house is on fire. Burt is only minutes away and gets to the house in a few minutes to extinguish the fire. Burt is freaked out that it could have been so much worse if the timing had been different. After evaluating the burn, he realizes it just melts some of the siding, and in the ashes, there is a cigarette butt left by Kaden. Burt goes inside the house, and Kaden walks upstairs with no shoes on. Burt tells him to get his shoes on, with Kaden replaying why he needs to. Burt screams, "Unless your name is Steven Seagal and you can kick my ass in bare feet, then get in the truck." When Burt and Kaden start driving out of the canyon with the backhoe, Kaden is really scared given how pissed off Burt is. Burt stops the truck and starts scolding Kaden, talking about trust, respect, and negligence on his property, telling him he is no longer allowed on the property until he can rebuild his trust.

Now the pages start to turn. Kaden seems to feel as though his world is gone; he's had fifteen years in this world, and at the blink of an eye, he fears it's gone. Kaden's attitude towards this act at a young age is something he can't control; his brain is not developed for such adulting. He starts fighting in school, hanging out at older kids' houses, and to top it all off, he gets caught with nicotine at school. He is suspended from school for a second time. Two suspensions per semester are all they allow for one year; Kaden is going to need to attend another school or drop out for an entire school year. The closest school is forty-five miles away, approximately a three-hour drive each day, which Burt cannot make happen. Kaden now has twenty-four hours of idle time; his days are now able to accept all kinds of wrongdoing, and there is not much Burt can do. Melissa can't take care of her own life, let alone another person, child or not. Kaden mixes in with a bad crowd; they like to party, they don't respect the law or have jobs, making a bad mix for young teenagers. Kaden gets talked into stealing checks out of Burt's house and cashing them at the local convenience store. Two or three boys cash the checks along with Kaden, posing as employees of Burt's business. One of the store's cashiers recognizes one of the boys as a convicted thief and calls the cops. They track down and question them about what they were doing. Kaden takes responsibility, and the police arrest him. He gets charged with forgery. Unfortunately, Kaden must go back to court for his charges, and just like the judge told him, he's going to juvenile detention for this arrest and the fact that he is kicked out of school for a year. The judge does not want him out on the street and gives him time equal to that of his return to school. They transport him to Twin Falls that day for a stay of seven months, and then a review of his progress.

Melissa is upset with Kaden; she can't believe he would do that along with Toto calling to confirm how Kaden has embarrassed the family once again. Melissa handles it by calling Burt and wants him to drop the charges, blaming him for making Kaden feel unwanted for smoking cigarettes. Melissa tells Burt she will attempt to get the house and vehicles in the divorce if he doesn't drop the charges. Burt explains to her that no matter what he does, Kaden will still have to spend seven months in juvenile detention because of his lack of school and not from his new charges. Melissa doesn't listen but understands Kaden will be down in Twin Falls no matter what anybody does; she'll deal with it. Over the next few months, Melissa and Burt don't talk much, having little in common, although Burt and William go to visit Kaden each week. On one Sunday during a parent visit, both Melissa and Burt show up at the same time. They get along fine but talk mainly with Kaden.

63

Melissa tells people about Burt's asinine Grizzley bear attitude, but it's Melissa who reacts explosively; perhaps it's because she lacks confidence in herself stemming from her childhood. Burt tells Melissa he will drop the charges and give her a vehicle if she promises to keep a close eye on Kaden. She agrees, and it's a decision Burt will regret for years to come.

Seven months pass, and Kaden is released from juvenile jail. He is happy to get out, although he feels pissed that he got sent there to start with, maybe even upset with Burt for not saving his ass. One afternoon, while sitting in the garage working on sleds, Kaden asks Burt if he would have left William in Twin Falls since he is his real son. Burt is pissed, not because he asks, but because he couldn't see the things that Burt has done for him and his mother — only two percent of what other humans receive from a friend on planet Earth. Burt tells him that he would do most anything for William, and he can't change the fact that Kaden is not his real son. Nothing legally, no amount of money, and no amount of praying will change it. Burt can't help but think that if Melissa had her shit together, they could have both lied about his father being Burt. After all, he has blue eyes, and everyone who met the boys would say that the boys are twins, and Kaden looks exactly like Burt. Nevertheless, Kaden can't help but think of the father he didn't know and seems to question whether his life would be better if he had one. Burt tells Kaden he doesn't know but will talk to his mom again, as the previous discussions have not yielded any results and perhaps it's a painful subject for her. Kaden starts to tear up, and Burt knows it's real for Kaden — that he yearns for the knowledge of his father, although Burt can't really do much. One afternoon, Burt receives a phone call from one of Kaden's girlfriends stating he has been breathing propane. She's worried and tells Burt she dropped him off at Melissa's house. Within a few weeks, Melissa struggles with controlling Kaden, mostly because he has lost all respect for her in raising him. They get into an argument, and she kicks him out of her house. Burt doesn't know the circumstances, but Kaden shows up late at night crying that his mom has told him to get out of her life. Burt tells him to go to bed and that they will talk about it in the morning. They go to bed, and Burt goes to work the next day. William calls Burt to tell him Kaden is in the garage acting weird; he is doing something with the race fuel. Burt hurries home to find Kaden huffing gasoline and nearly unconscious. He locks the garage and takes Kaden to the ER, where he is treated for carbon monoxide poisoning. Burt has a long talk with Kaden about destruction with things like this, explaining that it never goes uphill, it never makes things better, and if he doesn't get a grip on it, he will get Kaden into rehab.

Within a few weeks, Kaden has been staying at Burt's, hanging with William and William's stepsister. She has come up for a week before she goes to Italy for a year and will not be able to see Burt, William, or Kaden for a long time. Burt knows that Melissa feels abandoned, so he calls her to tell her she is welcome to come over to see Marie. She acknowledges she's welcome, but Burt feels as though she feels like the odd man out. Melissa usually coils up like a rattler when she gets this feeling; no one has taught her how to regulate her emotions, and it always goes back to her confidence or lack thereof. Burt has taken Marie to Ketchum late afternoon for lunch; it's the only time he can fit it into his busy schedule. Burt and Marie have a late lunch, and then Burt drives her to Folo's Photos to buy her a camera. She has no idea and freaks out that he is buying her an eighteen-hundred-dollar digital camera for her vacation. She goes back to Burt's house ecstatic and excited to take pictures and tells William that she wants to hike up and experiment with her new camera. William agrees to the hike to the top of the hill by the house but wants to be back by dark. They both agree and leave the house. Meanwhile, Kaden gets home, his mom showing up just minutes later. Kaden is playing video games in William's room. Melissa comes into the house and goes downstairs to see Kaden. When she enters William's room, she asks Kaden, "Whose truck is outside?" Kaden responds, "It is William's new truck." Melissa is upset with the new purchase; she feels like William is always getting his way and living a life of luxury. At that time, William and Marie walk in from the hike, and Melissa gives William a piece of her mind while she waits for Burt to get there. While Marie and Kaden are downstairs to avoid the argument, Marie realizes she doesn't have the camera in her bag; she has left it on top of the hill. She confides to Kaden that Burt just paid eighteen hundred dollars for it, and she must get it now, even though it's dark. William is freaked out by Melissa's aggressive attitude toward his belongings, so he sets his phone, laptop, and car keys on the counter while he and Marie go out to look for her camera. Meanwhile, Kaden tells Melissa that Burt just bought Marie an eighteen-hundred-dollar camera. Melissa has a meltdown—a nuclear meltdown—as Burt pulls into the driveway and makes his way to the house, hearing Melissa screaming before he gets to the front door. Burt can't believe his ears; he can't fathom his loved ones could even do that to him. Melissa screams at Burt that he knew she loved photography and wanted a nice camera like that. Burt blows up and says, "If I ever make any money, I will leave it all to Anna Nicole Smith."

In the next couple of days, Kaden has been complaining to Burt about headaches, but Burt figures it's from DT's and getting too much sleep. Kaden has been sleeping till noon every day. Burt tells Kaden and William to be ready to go to the gym at six o'clock in the evening, thinking this will get them back to health and establish a healthy schedule. Burt shows up, and the three of them go to the gym. Both boys aren't that happy to go; William is complaining he has homework, and Kaden has a headache. After a few minutes of working out in the bright lights, Kaden has a seizure and falls to the floor, and they rush him to the ER. After some time in the hospital, Kaden gets some medicine and a diagnosis of some kind of epilepsy. Over the next few months, Kaden has multiple seizures, with doctors increasing the dosage of his medication to make them stop. Both Burt and William think it's from the huffing of fuels.

Kaden has seizures a couple of times a week—usually one minor and one grand mal. He cannot function for hours after a big ten-minute seizure. Kaden realizes his condition and stops drinking or any substance that would make him have a seizure ever. Kaden can't get a driver's license, operate a gun, or ride toys with his new condition.

Melissa, for some reason, has a revelation that her son is going to die—maybe not now, but shortly if she doesn't help him. She starts going to AA and stops drinking. She stops by Burt's house to see everybody every couple of days, sometimes cooking dinner for Burt and the boys. Melissa apologizes to everybody for her actions; perhaps it's a step for AA, but nevertheless, she tries to make amends. She tells Burt that she loves him and that he was correct about her drinking and neglecting her son. Now she fears Kaden is in trouble. Melissa tells Burt that her sister Toto told her she would not be her sister anymore if she goes back to Burt, and she can accept that. Burt tells her he will have to think about it and will let her know after a few weeks go by.

Chapter 15 – Dreams

Weeks go by, and Melissa continues to stop by and do things for the boys. At one time, she shows Burt and the boys a calendar indicating how far she has gone without drinking. Melissa is proud of herself, even though she doesn't act like it. Burt can tell she struggles to keep her calendar going. She tells Burt she always thought he only wanted to marry her because she was pregnant and that afterward, he didn't even love or care about her. Burt explains she is crazy as a loon, that nobody does the things he does when they don't care for someone. Melissa agrees and starts to cry. She exclaims she has lost most of her family and she isn't even very old; she's only thirty-five. Burt tells her there is plenty of time to rekindle her relationship with her son, but what will be a struggle is parting ways with her drinking friends. It's just not possible for most humans to keep addictive people around and stay sober. Melissa agrees, thinking that she can do it while knowing the difficult road ahead of her.

Burt stops by Melissa's house and asks if she wants to have lunch the next day. Melissa agrees and explains she is at a new location for work, as the old place was getting her down. Burt laughs and says, "What number is this?" Melissa smiles and says it's only four. The next day, Burt picks her up at work for lunch, and they proceed to a restaurant. Burt tells her he knew she had a tough upbringing and that she missed her parents, but it is something he cannot fix. He can try to ease her mind over himself not loving her, and if she wants, he will take her to Hawaii as he knows they never had a honeymoon. She is excited. "It's Hawaii!" In a couple of weeks, when work slows down for the fall, they will go without the boys. It will be just time to enjoy life without worrying about friends or family.

It is winter in McCall, and both Burt and Melissa are off to Hawaii. The boys stay with relatives. Twenty days in the sun on the beach without drinks or drama. Melissa gets to have dinner, watch swimming fish, run on the beach, all without being intoxicated. Melissa and Burt go to a nice restaurant to enjoy a good meal when they are approached by a Polynesian girl who asks if Burt wants to purchase a flower for Melissa's hair for ten dollars. Burt agrees, and the young lady starts weaving the flower into her hair. Moments later, the girl approaches another man and his date to ask the same question. The other couple is really intoxicated and not getting along very well for the evening. The man snaps at the young lady, "Do you have any stinging nettle or poison ivy for my wife?" His wife storms out. Both Burt and Melissa laugh and acknowledge alcohol probably caused it. A vacation very well deserved for both, for the union as a whole, and for the elimination of alcohol. They return from Hawaii rejuvenated and ready for the future of the family.

On the Homefront, things move forward. William excels in school and has a job at a local restaurant. Kaden gets a job at the ski hill, and Melissa makes it six months without drinking. Melissa struggles without her friends, even though some of her friends stop by to chat occasionally. They understand she is trying to remain sober, but people all struggle with life and its challenges; misery loves company, as they say. Burt and Melissa don't get invited to get-togethers, birthday parties, and functions that involve alcohol. It would be a problem for Burt, but Melissa finds it impossible. It is a sad friendship built on such things as addiction, and it is also sad that it breaks down because of the lack of it. Melissa teams up with an elderly woman from work, a confidante on her journey, who takes her under her wing and teaches her the skill of title work.

Melissa spends her empty time with Marla, learning all about the business of housing title work. Marla raised her children years earlier, so Marla helps Melissa with title, escrow, and life in general without alcohol. Marla treats her as a second daughter, even though Marla probably doesn't like Burt that much. She respects him for what Burt is—a father. Melissa works hard to reach a point of being called a title officer and making three times the money. She secures a life without alcohol. Marla is a good fit for Melissa during this time.

Melissa starts to gain a reputation for her ability in thorough title searches, complete background data, and quick service, mostly because she puts in extra time after work while others leave at five o'clock. Melissa fights each day to remain sober; it is tough work with her DNA and twenty years of abuse, but she battles her own struggles well. Burt is proud of her, and she confides in Burt that life is really boring without alcohol. Burt assures her that she will find it less boring in time. Melissa's boss is proud of the work she produces and says that once Marla retires in a few months, Melissa will take her place if things go right. Melissa's boss wants her to attend as many meetings and seminars as she can to advance her knowledge. Melissa agrees, as she has her eyes set on Marla's job in six months or so. It gives her her own office, more money, and the versatility to have a career. She goes to seminars in Boise, Pocatello, and smaller meetings across the state to advance her career knowledge. She attends them with her boss and some other employees; they usually are one- to two-day workshops/seminars with the crew staying overnight in the motel that hosts the event.

It has been almost a year of sobriety for Melissa. She has done very well, but her strength is never impervious. She fights the battle every day and has now gone almost a year without friends — friends who were fun and loved to party. Melissa has built a barrier to shield herself from hearing about what is going on without her in the group. The only contact she has about things and people is her sister, Toto, and Toto has shut her out for years for embarrassing the family. Things are different now; her sister Toto and her husband are on the rocks, and she wants her sister to party with her. This causes a large problem between Burt and Toto; they lock horns more than once about his family and hers. Toto calls him a control freak,

Burt calls her short, fat, $#@%, and that makes the tension all the worse for Melissa and her sobriety. Toto has never really liked Burt; they have always clashed in views, but Toto's husband usually sets things straight with other people she's tangled with. He is not going to tango with Burt at six-foot-four and two-fifty pounds. He has tried and lost before. Besides, Toto's husband is irritated by her drinking, getting drunk all the time, and wrecking her car. Toto has always been the responsible one, and now the table has turned. Toto wants Melissa down in the dumps with her. Melissa calls Burt on the way home and asks him to meet her at a bar and help her with her sister, as Toto is really drunk at the local hangout. Burt agrees to meet her but really doesn't want any involvement with helping Toto at all. However, he climbs into his truck anyway and heads to the bar. Upon reaching the bar parking lot, Melissa is screaming, and Burt comes over to find a man on top of Toto in the seat of a pickup truck. Burt pulls the man out of the truck and escorts Toto to his truck and then back home to her place. Melissa has choice words for her sister as Burt drives Toto home—a harsh scolding that will haunt her in later months.

Addicts struggle every day with things that non-addicts don't even know exist. While work is what so many worry about for the day, addicts have a list of things to steer them through each day of life—work or not. Each day is a different route to success, something that most humans try to stay away from, be it drinking or drugs, as getting out alive is a battle with few wins. The Giles family struggles every day with these monkeys; they are all subject to the horrible life of addiction. While most families deal with raising cats, puppies, and maybe a horse, the Giles are herding monkeys, and they are riding their backs at an early age. Burt works every day to keep the monkeys at bay with his family—no booze in the house, boys are not allowed to drink, including Burt—trying to keep Melissa and the boys clean. Most of Burt and Melissa's friends find it weird, commenting, "Who doesn't have alcohol in their house?" All the while, they have problems in their own families. Burt lectures the boys, William and Kaden, about drugs and alcohol every chance he gets, usually while camping, hiking, or hunting. Burt's goal is to never allow the kids to start in the first place. It is a battle for any parent, let alone a family who finds addiction as normal. Melissa, for whatever reason in her past or present mind, does what Burt would never allow nor dream of when she purchases beer for her son, Kaden—something the two, Burt and Melissa, fight about on occasions. Burt suspects that Kaden and William have not only genetic genes for addiction but also social addiction, which drives Burt to try and eliminate them from their young lives. People, including parents, struggle with the fact that their kids might become better people and possibly excel past their own success. Jealousy comes to fight. Perhaps Melissa is fighting this battle as well, and Toto is fighting her own embarrassment with the exposed family hardships. It is hard to go three steps forward and two steps back for anyone.

Melissa's success is one to be admired. She is sober, has a high-paying job, and a good life with money to look happy and beautiful each day. Melissa has beaten alcohol for almost one year, which, other than jail time, is a record for her family tree. But one little thing can throw off that success. Melissa continues to strive in her job, but sometimes maybe she shouldn't go any farther without a safety net—nets limit achievements. One comedian states in a humorous way that sometimes people live too long, meaning just that: if we could just pause our life movie at the good spots. Melissa attends a seminar with her boss in Idaho Falls one week. They leave early one day and sit through long sessions of the title business. After having dinner, they retire to their rooms. Melissa calls Burt to see what he is up to; they talk for a while, say goodbye, and agree to speak the next day. The next day, the sessions are a little shorter, and after a good night's sleep, the crew is up in the lounge of the motel. Some are just talking, some are having a few drinks. Melissa is out of her element—her safety net. Melissa's boss offers her a drink, and she accepts. It is her boss, and like any addict, what could one drink hurt? The two continue to hang out until most of the lounge has cleared out. Melissa is really intoxicated, and to her boss, she is a young beautiful woman; his judgment is also altered by lust and alcohol. Burt tries to call that evening until late in the night with no answer. He gets worried about her and has the motel page her room. Again, no answer, so Burt explains to the front desk that he is worried and asks if they can check again in the morning. They agree. The next day, Burt calls the desk again, and they say Melissa has asked the front desk to call her a cab as she is sick and going to the ER. A couple of hours later, she answers her phone and says she is on her way home and will talk when she arrives as they have decided to come home early from the seminar.

Chapter 16 – The Split

Burt knows the drill, but for the sake of family, he waits until he finds the truth. When Melissa arrives home, Burt can tell she's sick from alcohol. There's no talking to Melissa when she's this sick; she needs to sleep it off for a day, so waiting is the best remedy. Burt is upset, but before he passes judgment on things, he must get the facts. Burt remembers he's kind of an asshole. He calls Melissa's boss's house. His wife answers the phone, and they begin to talk as her husband takes a nap.

"I'm just trying to figure out what happened to Melissa. Should I be concerned about her ER visit? It must have been bad if she went to her boss's room at five AM to call for a cab. Perhaps she was lucky enough they had adjoining rooms," Burt says.

"Thank you," his wife replies before hanging up. An hour or so later, the boss's wife calls back, wishing to speak to the drunk whore. Burt can tell she is very, very upset, although he informs her that Melissa is passed out. Burt senses that Melissa's boss has also left doubt in his wife's mind, as his phone was out of service during the evening.

Later, Melissa's boss admits he slept with Melissa. They both got too drunk and ended up in his room; it was just a mistake of judgment. An hour later, the son of Melissa's boss calls Burt, screaming that he is causing his parents to get a divorce. Burt wonders how he is to blame for this affair but eagerly embraces the title triumphantly.

The next couple of days get extremely tough for Melissa. Things are crashing down, and they crash hard. Melissa builds walls as fast as she can; she has the most to lose in her life and doesn't have any place to turn. Melissa goes to work on Monday, hoping it's all a dream, but it isn't. Most of the office knows, and her worst nightmare—the boss—is there. The temperature is more than she can handle; it has always been easier to just disappear, but where would she go? Melissa calls her friend, and Marla suggests she call the owner of the title company and ask if she can transfer to another town, as she knows that would get her out of the heat. Going to another company in town won't be enough. Melissa calls the owner, asking for a job, and he informs her that she can transfer to Sandpoint. Melissa now has a job on Tuesday the following week. She just needs to get things settled on the home front, and she isn't sure how that will be. Melissa knows Burt is good to her; she knows he is done with her and how much hate he has built up in fourteen years. Which direction will he turn? She goes home to Burt, knowing she needs to be professional. He doesn't play into games; it is her last chance.

Melissa informs Burt that she must leave him, leave the valley, and leave her family, and if possible, she could use Burt's help. Melissa explains that she knows it's her fault, but she just can't be sober forever, and that will always haunt her and her family. She tells Burt that if he gives her a new truck titled in her name with no business logo and allows her to keep her married last name, she will leave town quietly and sign divorce papers. At this time, Burt agrees. The next day, Burt goes to town, purchases a truck, and has divorce papers drawn up. He returns home to prepare for the large family camping trip he's going on the next day. It's Labor Day weekend, and Burt and his brother Jonathan have planned it for months. The boys are excited to go. Melissa comes by later to seal the deal, pick up the new vehicle, and say goodbye to the boys as they leave with Burt early in the morning for the planned camping trip. Melissa and Burt part ways, both knowing it's time, but not before Melissa and her friends feel justified in theft. The day before Melissa leaves, she goes by Burt's home with her friends. While Burt is on a family vacation, Melissa loads up the things she feels justified to own. The girls load up guns, pictures, and other household items she feels she can use for her new place up north. It's illegal, but Burt writes it off as fair in love and war. Melissa hits the road with a full truck as she is on borrowed time to keep her sister and friends from wanting an explanation for what is going on with her — something Melissa is not prepared to do, let alone explain to her boss's wife.

Burt tells the boys it has been a tough year and that he has purchased a cruise for just him and the boys. Burt tells the boys to get all their IDs, wallets, money, and clothes ready to take off in the next day or two. Burt gathers his things and even remembers to bring extra IDs for the boys, just in case. Burt and the boys have a great time driving to Los Angeles and then spending a day at Disneyland to play in the park. The three of them are having a great time until Kaden gets kicked out for smoking cigarettes in the park. Kaden must borrow a phone from security and call Burt, who is on a ride with William. Since he has been kicked out for smoking, Burt will have to repurchase a ticket to get him back inside the gates at a cost of ninety dollars. Burt is pissed and tells Kaden, "I will rip your lips off if you do it again," which Kaden hears after judging Burt's attitude.

The next day, Burt and the boys leave the motel and head thirty miles to the boat dock for boarding the three-day cruise ship. As check-in begins, Burt has all the information for Kaden and for William to board except for William's ID. William then realizes he has left his wallet in the motel thirty miles away, and there is not enough time to drive there and back before the cruise boat sets sail. Burt freaks out that William cannot board the ship but talks to a cruise attendant. They suggest calling the police to verify it is "him." They do that, and the officer tells William he will do it for him but must inform William that if he has any warrants, he will be arrested on site. It works, and William is allowed to board the ship. They all get their luggage ready. Kaden, who has just an old army bag for his trip, is the only luggage that makes it onto the ship, as some other passengers and Burt/William's suitcases are two of the ones that don't. By the grace of God, William takes his laptop and other valuables in his carry-on, as nothing else is on the ship as it sails out of the harbor. Burt and William contact the front desk, and they inform them that some passengers' luggage fell overboard while loading the ship. The luggage is guaranteed for two hundred fifty dollars each, and they hand Burt and William a couple of free T-shirts to wear for the rest of the trip, crediting them for the five hundred-dollar loss. The cruise is fascinating to the boys; they care little about clothes and start exploring the ship. It's huge, and you can't get lost. The next day, they go on an excursion to Ensenada, Mexico City, and walk through miles of flea markets, purchasing a few items. All three purchase some souvenirs for people back home. Kaden even borrows twenty dollars for some glass pipes in the shape of a whale. About an hour later, the policía approaches Burt and the family. Burt asks what the stop is about. The policía informs Burt that after watching Kaden, they suspect he has drugs on him. Kaden informs them he does not; he only bought two little whale pipes for his friends back home. They beg to differ and tell Burt they will need to strip search him or he will be arrested. Burt doesn't want any arrests to take place in Mexico, so he agrees. They inform Kaden to take all his clothes off while just standing in the public eye — in a public parking lot with people gathering around to witness the commotion. After the search is over, they tell Burt that they are good to go; they were just taking precautions. Kaden puts his clothes back on. They return to the ship. Burt is upset with Mexico and its police force, but they go to the diner, brush it off, and have a great time that evening. By the cruise's end and final checkout payment, Burt learns that Kaden has charged seventeen hundred twenty dollars in alcohol to his room. Burt is pissed but pays it, blaming himself for allowing the charges as this is his first cruise and he didn't know the drinking age was eighteen or he would have watched Kaden closer. Kaden knows Burt is steaming pissed off and doesn't say a word on the way home, only calling his mom, Melissa. He tells her that he bought all the girls on the boat drinks and didn't think it would be that much on a three-day cruise.

Melissa moves to Sandpoint, hoping to do it right once again. Everyone at work loves her, feels sorry for her, and thinks she is the most beautiful girl in town. For Melissa, it's like she has found Paradise Valley, thinking perhaps alcohol isn't addictive, jealous women won't hate her, and the law is forgiving. Every place she goes, men are nice to her; nobody knows her past. She has no baggage—it's probably the only time in her life nobody knows her name, doesn't know she's Native American, that she's been married, that she's not wanted by police, and she's not hated by fellow employees. She has very little stress in her life currently—a great job, no bills, a high credit score, and for the first time in eighteen years, no child to take care of. Life is great, although with all the excitement, she still loves her friends and misses them somewhat. Melissa wonders if her friends can run up north, as she doesn't ever want to return to McCall.

Melissa calls her sister and asks if she and some of the girls want to run to North Idaho for her birthday, as she hasn't partied with them for over a year. Toto talks to the girls—the girls who are all alcoholics, struggling with life, struggling with their own marriages—and each of them plans to attend the birthday party. New meat in town is always fun until somebody must pay the piper, and only time will tell. Melissa's birthday comes, and the girls roll up to Sandpoint to party, having a wonderful time and getting their fix of partying with new and old drinking buddies. "The grass is always greener on the other side of the fence," right? As the piper would have it, a few weeks later, two girls file for divorce—one being Melissa's sister Toto—and one has developed an STD. But for Melissa, it went quite well; she has found a boyfriend. He works at a factory and could use help if Melissa knows of anybody who needs a job. Melissa calls Kaden and tells him he can always move to North Idaho with her if things get to the point where he wants to leave. Melissa is feeling a little lonely, and she feels the next time around, she can handle parenting Kaden.

Chapter 17 – The Blame

Back at the valley, things don't get better for young adults; chaos continues. Boys being boys, one weekend out partying around a campfire, the boys start talking about girls, and that leads into mothers. One boy brings up MILFs, and they start naming some of the mothers in the valley they would have an affair with. As with all locker room talk, one boy brings up the attractive girl who contracted the STD from the party in Sandpoint. All the boys laugh and joke about how she's hot and cold. One of those boys at the campfire kills himself a few weeks later in the same canyon. Burt never knows the reason, just that he was friends with the group.

Melissa calls Kaden and asks him if he has thought about moving to North Idaho and working at the factory; Kaden could live with her as she has a two-bedroom house. Kaden decides he will try it, as he has been laid off at the ski hill, and the factory has shifts for twenty-four hours. Melissa travels to McCall, picks up Kaden, loads up his ATV and his hunting rifles, spends some time with friends and her nieces, and drives back up north. Kaden enjoys being up north; it's a small area, and he can ride his ATV to and from work, to hunting and fishing spots, keeping him on time for the swing shift. The swing shift is made for Kaden; he can sleep till noon every day and get done at midnight, late enough not to get in trouble. Kaden is doing quite well; he misses Burt and William and calls about every other day to chat. Burt and Kaden have thousands of hours of memories, and Kaden misses that—something his mother cannot replace. The bond they have is strong. Burt has never let him down; he's been the rock that Kaden knows is there come rain or shine. Kaden talks to Burt constantly about finding his real father and fights quite commonly with his mother about it. It is something he really can't understand with his mother and her wanting to hide it from him. It's something that Burt has no knowledge of and doesn't really know how much it truly bothers Kaden. It's something he has tried to ask but starts a war with Melissa. Burt has even asked Melissa's best friends at one time about the topic, but it started a huge problem with Burt and Melissa's friends, so for Burt, it's best to let it go.

Melissa continues to drink and party, staying at her boyfriend's house on the weekends, limiting the fighting with Kaden about not keeping the house clean. Kaden's disrespect creates a huge crevasse in their relationship, especially for a mother and child. Melissa has created this, but Burt's attitude of drinking hasn't helped her relationship with Kaden; he bounces from right to wrong. Melissa stays over at her boyfriend more often when Melissa and Kaden are fighting about things. It doesn't solve the problem, but it keeps the flames down. Kaden finds that going to the gym and working out before work keeps him fitter and less likely to be at home so much. He can work out and shower at the gym, keeping any mess away from Melissa's house, making their relationship better. Burt and his brother are very close; Burt's brother is better at talking with Kaden because Jonathan has had his own battles with drugs and alcohol. Kaden loves to reminisce about stories with Burt and Jonathan and can go on forever, inciting a new story. Kaden calls one day on Burt's mobile truck phone while both Burt and Jonathan are in the truck going to a job site. Kaden is very happy to talk to both at the same time. Burt teases him, "Only benching two hundred pounds?" Kaden laughs and says he can't believe an old guy benches that much. Kaden knows Burt thinks he's tough, as Burt has told other people, and accepts he has years to go to gain that strength. He talks about moving back down to McCall, working out with Burt and Jonathan again, but Burt tells him he has a great job and is doing fine in Sandpoint. Kaden is in a good mood as he leaves the gym, getting to talk on the phone and heading to work for the swing shift, one he enjoys by getting off at midnight. Kaden is quite happy with his situation—making money, and working a job he can keep because they offer a swing shift, something he wouldn't have in McCall.

After work, Kaden heads home on his ATV and arrives at Melissa's house at about the same time as his mom. She has been at the bar and is intoxicated. Kaden exclaims, "It's the first time I've seen you in a few days, and you've been drinking with friends rather than checking on me." Melissa and Kaden start arguing about drinking and parenting, but mainly because she's drunk. Kaden tries to get under her skin as he feels it will help solve the problem of her alcoholism. Everybody knows, including Melissa, that it won't, but he's young and feels humiliation will make it stop. Melissa's MO is to get aggressive about her neglect, but her aggression this time isn't really about a dirty house. It's that she's lost her job as the housing economy is tanking, and she's taking it out on anyone close. The housing market is slowing down to a crawl, and employees are getting laid off in the title business. Because of the flood of applicants, employers are asking for resumes, and Melissa doesn't have a high school diploma. In a busy economy, it wouldn't matter, but times are different now, and employers only need the best applicants. Perhaps working on a GED or equivalent during her party times could have saved her job. Melissa is angry and probably depressed about having to go back to cleaning or waitressing after losing her title job. Melissa has always struggled with the blame game. Rather than facing up to her own mistakes, she tries to blame life on others around her. Kaden just happens to be the piñata for the night, but when would the wrong place, wrong time fit your own child? For some reason, with all the name-calling, bashing, and screaming, Kaden starts crying. This empowers Melissa. She tells him to cry upstairs. It's kind of a family saying Melissa and Toto always use for manning up, suggesting putting on your big girl panties—a phrase Burt always thought was ridiculous, as if adulting was the goal. "Wouldn't you rise above the issue?"

Kaden retreats upstairs, where his bedroom is located, and slams the door. Melissa continues to clean the kitchen, trying to fight off the reality of where her life is going now. She is a little taken aback by Kaden's reaction. Most of the time, he goes off somewhere to allow the situation to cool down. It isn't like it's their first argument or the only time she's been intoxicated. A few minutes later, Melissa hears Kaden screaming loudly and what she thinks is a gunshot. She runs upstairs and is correct.

Kaden is dead!